# COOKING FOR TODDLERS

# COOKING
# FOR TODDLERS

## How to give your toddler the best
## health and vitality

## SARA LEWIS

HERMES
HOUSE

This edition is published by Hermes House, an imprint of Anness Publishing Ltd, Hermes House, 88–89 Blackfriars Road, London SE1 8HA
tel. 020 7401 2077; fax 020 7633 9499
www.hermeshouse.com; www.annesspublishing.com

If you like the images in this book and would like to investigate using them for publishing, promotions or advertising, please visit our website
www.practicalpictures.com for more information.

Publisher: Joanna Lorenz
Editorial Director: Judith Simons
Project Editors: Emma Wish, Molly Perham and Richard McGinlay
Designer: Sue Storey
Special Photography: John Freeman
Stylist: Judy Williams
Home Economists: Sara Lewis, Jacqueline Clarke and Petra Jackson

## ETHICAL TRADING POLICY

Because of our ongoing ecological investment programme, you, as our customer, can have the pleasure and reassurance of knowing that a tree is being cultivated on your behalf to naturally replace the materials used to make the book you are holding. For further information about this scheme, go to **www.annesspublishing.com/trees**

Previously published as *What to Feed Your Toddler*

### PUBLISHER'S NOTE

Although the advice and information in this book are believed to be accurate and true at the time of going to press, neither the authors nor the publisher can accept any legal responsibility or liability for any errors or omissions that may be made nor for any inaccuracies nor for any loss, harm or injury that comes about from following instructions or advice in this book.

### NOTES

• Bracketed terms are intended for American readers.
• For all recipes, quantities are given in both metric and imperial measures and, where appropriate, in standard cups and spoons. Follow one set, but not a mixture, because they are not interchangeable.
• Standard spoon and cup measures are level. 1 tsp = 5ml, 1 tbsp = 15ml, 1 cup = 250ml/8fl oz.
• Australian standard tablespoons are 20ml. Australian readers should use 3 tsp in place of 1 tbsp for measuring small quantities of gelatine, flour, salt, etc.
• American pints are 16fl oz/2 cups. American readers should use 20fl oz/2.5 cups in place of 1 pint when measuring liquids.
• Electric oven temperatures in this book are for conventional ovens. When using a fan oven, the temperature will probably need to be reduced by about 10–20°C/20–40°F. Since ovens vary, you should check with your manufacturer's instruction book for guidance.
• Medium (US large) eggs are used unless otherwise stated.

### ACKNOWLEDGEMENTS

• The Department of Health
• National Dairy Council Nutrition Service
• Healthy Education Authority
• Dr Nigel Dickie from Heinz Baby Foods
• The British Dietetic Association
• The Health Visitors Association
• For Broadstone Communications for their invaluable help supplying Kenwood equipment for recipe testing and photography
• Hand-painted china plates, bowls and mugs from Cosmo Place Studio
• Tupperware for plain-coloured plastic bowls, plates, feeder beakers and cups
• Cole and Mason for children's ware
• Royal Doulton for Bunnykins china
• Spode for blue and white Edwardian Childhood china

### PICTURE CREDITS

Bubbles: page 11 br (Jacqui Farrow); pages 9 t, 10 t (Ian West).
Reflections/Jennie Woodcock: pages 11 br, 19 br, 48 br, 78 br.
(Key: t = top; b = bottom; r = right.)

# CONTENTS

# INTRODUCTION

Once your child has reached 12 months he or she will be enjoying a varied diet, and eating habits and their personal food preferences will be developing. It is now vitally important to lay the foundations of a good and well-balanced eating regime.

This is a time when food fads may also develop. Try to weather this period of fussy eating – all children will experience it at some time, and even good eaters will go through a picky stage. Hopefully, the fad will go as quickly as it came, but while it lasts, meal-times can become a nightmare.

# A Balanced and Varied Diet

Give your child a selection of foods in the four main food groups daily:

**Cereal and filler foods:** include three to four helpings of the following per day – breakfast cereals, bread, pasta, potatoes, rice.

**Fruit and vegetables:** try to have three or four helpings per day. Choose from fresh, canned, frozen or dried.

**Meat and/or alternatives:** one to two portions per day – meat (all kinds, including burgers and sausages), poultry, fish (fresh, canned or frozen), eggs (well cooked), lentils, peas and beans (for example, chickpeas baked beans, red kidney beans), finely chopped nuts, smooth peanut butter, seeds, tofu, and Quorn.

**Dairy foods:** include 600ml/1 pint of milk per day or a mix of milk, cheese, and yogurt. For a child who stops drinking milk, try flavouring it or using it in custards, ice cream, rice pudding or cheese sauce. A carton of yogurt or 40g/1½oz of cheese have the same amount of calcium as 190ml/⅓ pint of milk.

### THE IMPORTANCE OF BREAKFAST

Breakfast is a vitally important start for any young child. Count back: your child may have had a meal at 5 o'clock the previous day, and if she misses breakfast at 8 o'clock she will not have eaten for 15 hours. Allow time to sit down, and don't rush your child. Offer milk and cereals, orange juice diluted with a little water, not squash (orangeade), a few slices of fruit and half a piece of toast, preferably spread with smooth peanut butter or Marmite.

Above: *Cereal and filler foods, such as bread, pasta and rice.*

Above: *Fruit and vegetables, including frozen, dried and canned goods.*

Above: *Meat and meat alternatives, such as beans, peas, lentils and nuts.*

Above: *Dairy foods such as milk, cheese and yogurt.*

**Marmite toast**

**Sliced pears**

## FATS

As adults we are all aware of the need to cut down on our fat consumption, but when eating together as a family, bear in mind that fat is a useful source of energy in a child's diet. The energy from fat is in concentrated form, so that your child can take in the calories she needs for growth and development before her stomach becomes overfull. Fat in food is also a valuable source of the fat-soluble vitamins, A, D, E and K, as well as essential fatty acids that the body cannot make by itself.

In general, fat is best provided by foods that contain not just fat but other essential nutrients as well, such as dairy products, eggs, meat and fish. Full-fat (whole) milk and its products such as cheese and yogurt, and eggs contain the fat-soluble vitamins A and D, while sunflower (sunflower-seed) oil, nuts and oily fish are a good source of various essential fatty acids.

It is wise to cut down on deep frying and to grill (broil) or oven bake foods where possible. All children love crisps (potato chips), but keep them as a treat rather than a daily snack.

Above: *Keep sweets and chocolate as treats – give fruit and vegetables as snacks.*

## FRUIT AND VEGETABLES

Fresh fruit and vegetables play an essential part in a balanced diet. Offer fresh fruit, such as slices of apple or banana, for breakfast and the evening meal, and perhaps thin sticks of raw carrot and celery for lunch. Instead of biscuits (cookies), offer your child raisins, apricots, satsumas, carrots or apple slices if she wants a mid-morning or afternoon snack. Keep the fruit bowl within easy reach so your child may be tempted to pick up a banana as she walks through the kitchen.

Above: *A good mixture of the four basic food types will provide maximum energy and vitality for growing children.*

## SNACKS

Young children cannot eat enough food at meal-times to meet their needs for energy and growth, and snacks can play a vital part in meeting these needs. However, keep biscuits and crisps as a treat. They contain little goodness and are bad for the teeth. At meal-times keep sweets (candy) out of sight until the main course has been eaten.

**Bread sticks**

**Raisins**

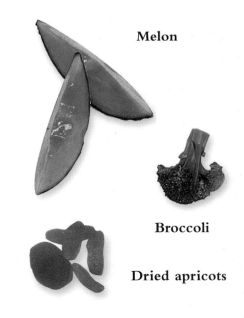

**Melon**

**Broccoli**

**Dried apricots**

# Coping With a Fussy Eater

We all have different sized appetites whatever our age, and young children are no exception. Children's appetites fluctuate greatly and often tail off just before a growth spurt. All children go through food fads; some just seem to last longer and be more difficult than others.

A toddler's appetite varies enormously, and you may find that she will eat very well one day and eat hardly anything the next. Be guided by your toddler, and try to think in terms of what the child has eaten over several days rather than just concentrating on one day.

At the time, it can be very frustrating and worrying. Try not to think of the food that you have just thrown away, but try to think more in the long term. Jot down the foods that your child has actually eaten over three or four days, or up to a week. You may actually be surprised that it isn't just yogurts and crisps (US potato chips) after all!

Once you have a list, you may find a link between the foods your child eats and the time of day. Perhaps your child eats better when eating with the family, or when the house is quiet. If you do find a link, then build on it. You might find that your child is snacking on chocolate, doughnuts or soft drinks when out with friends, and that fussiness at home is really a full tummy. Or it may be that by cutting out a milk drink and a biscuit (cookie) mid-morning and offering a sliced apple instead, your child may not be so full at lunchtime. Perhaps you could hide the biscuit tin (cookie jar) once visitors have had one, so that tiny hands can't keep reaching for more.

If your toddler seems hungrier at breakfast, then you could offer French toast, a grilled sausage or a few banana slices with her cereal.

Above: *Don't panic about food rejection. Be patient and keep a journal listing what your child actually does eat.*

Right: *Fresh, healthy snacks of fruit, such as apples, will preserve your child's appetite for main meals.*

Although this may all sound very obvious, when rushing about caring for a toddler and perhaps an older child or new baby as well, life can become rather blurred, and it can be difficult to stand back and look at things objectively.

**REFUSING TO EAT**

A child will always eat if she is hungry, although it may not be when you want her to eat. A child can stay fit and healthy on surprisingly little. Providing your child is growing and gaining weight, then don't fuss, but if you are worried, talk to your doctor or health visitor. Take the lead from your child, never force feed a child and try not to let meal-times become a battleground.

## MAKING MEAL-TIMES FUN

Coping with a fussy eater can be incredibly frustrating. The less she eats, the crosser you get, and so the spiral goes on as your toddler learns how to control meal-times. To break this vicious circle, try diffusing things by involving your child in the preparation of the meal. You could pack up a picnic with your child's help, choosing together what to take. Then go somewhere different to eat — it could be the back garden, the swings or even the car. Alternatively, have a dollies' or teddies' tea party or make a camp under the dining table or even in the cupboard under the stairs.

Even very young children enjoy having friends round for tea. If your child is going through a fussy or non-eating stage, invite over a little friend with a good appetite. Try to take a back seat, and don't make a fuss over how much the visiting child eats compared to your own.

Above: *Changing the scene and breaking routine can help greatly.*

Below: *Making the meal a special event can distract the child from any eating worries.*

Above: *Getting your child to help you cook the food will encourage her to eat it, too.*

Above: *Children are more likely to eat with friends of their own age around them.*

## 10 TIPS TO COPE WITH A FUSSY EATER

**1** Try to find meals that the rest of the family enjoys and where there are at least one or two things the fussy child will eat, as well. It may seem easier to cook only foods that your child will eat, but it means a very limited diet for everyone else, and your child will never get the chance to have a change of mind and try something new.

**2** Serve smaller portions of food to your child.

**3** Invite round her friend with a hearty appetite. A good example sometimes works, but don't comment on how much the visiting child has eaten.

**4** Invite an adult who the child likes for supper – a granny, uncle or friend. Sometimes a child will eat for someone else without any fuss at all.

**5** Never force feed a child.

**6** If your child is just playing with the food and won't eat, quietly remove the plate without a fuss and don't offer dessert.

**7** Try to make meal-times enjoyable and talk about what the family has been doing.

**8** Try limiting snacks and drinks between meals so your child feels hungrier when it comes to family meal-times. Alternatively, offer more nutritious snacks and smaller main meals if your child eats better that way.

**9** Offer drinks after a meal so that they don't spoil the appetite.

**10** Offer new foods when you know your child is hungry and hopefully more receptive.

Above: *Remember to give drinks after the meal, not before.*

## EATING TOGETHER

Sharing meals as a family should be a happy part of the day, but can turn into a nightmare if everyone is tired or you feel as though the only things your children will eat are chips (french fries). There is nothing worse than preparing a lovely supper, laying the table and sitting down with everyone, and then one child refuses to eat, shrieks her disapproval or just pushes the food around the plate. However hard you try to ignore this behaviour, the meal is spoiled for everyone, especially if this is a regular occurrence. It's not fair on you or anyone else.

If you feel this is just a passing phase, then you could try just ignoring it and carry on regardless. Try to praise the good things, perhaps the way the child sits nicely at the table or the way she holds a knife and fork. Talk about the things that have been happening during the day, rather than concentrating on the meal itself. Try to avoid comparing your child's appetite with more hearty eaters. With luck, this particular fad will go away.

However, if it becomes a regular thing and meal-times always seem more like a battleground than a happy family gathering, perhaps it's time for a more serious approach.

### First steps

• Check to see if there is something physically wrong with your child. Has she been ill? If she has, she may not have recovered fully. If you're worried, then ask your doctor.
• Perhaps your child has enlarged adenoids or tonsils which could make swallowing difficult, or perhaps she has a food allergy, such as coeliacs disease – an intolerance to gluten, which may be undiagnosed, but which would give the child tummy pains after eating. Again, check with your doctor.
• Is your child worried or stressed? If your family circumstances have changed – the arrival of a new baby, or if you've moved recently – your child may be unhappy or confused.
• Is your child trying to get your attention?

Above: *Good seating of the right height will contribute to comfort and relaxation.*

**Secondly**

Look at the way in which you as a family eat. Do you eat at regular times? Do you sit down to eat or catch snacks on the move? Do you enjoy your food, or do you always feel rushed and harassed? Children will pick up habits from their parents – bad ones as well as good. If you don't tend to sit down to a meal, or you have the habit of getting up during meal-times to do other jobs, then it's hard to expect your child to behave differently.

**Finally**

Talk things over with the whole family. If you all feel enough is enough, then it's time to make a plan of action. Explain that from now on you are all going to eat together where possible, when and where you say so. You will choose the food, there will be three meals a day and no snacks. Since milk is filling and dulls the appetite, milky drinks will only be given after a meal; during the meal water or juice will be provided.

It is important to involve the entire family in this strategy so that there is no dipping into the biscuit tin (cookie jar) or raiding the cupboard for crisps (potato chips) after school. Make sure that the fussy eater is aware of what is going to happen and give a few days' notice so that the idea can sink in.

Once you have outlined your strategy, work out your menus and

**Happy Families**

stick to them. Include foods your child definitely likes, chicken or carrots for instance, and obviously avoid foods your child dislikes although you could introduce some new foods for variety. Set yourself a time scale, perhaps one or two weeks, and review things after this period has elapsed.

**PUTTING THE PLAN INTO ACTION**

Begin your new plan of action when the entire family is there to help, such as a weekend, and stick to it. Make a fuss of the plans so it seems more like a game than a prison sentence. Add a few flowers to the table or a pretty cloth to make it more special.

Begin the day with a normal breakfast, but give the fussy eater the smallest possible portion. If the child eats it up, then offer something you know your child likes, such as an apple, a few raisins or a fruit yogurt.

As the days progress, you could offer a biscuit (cookie) or milkshake as a treat.

Give plenty of encouragement and praise, but be firm if the child plays up. If she behaves badly, take her to a different room or to the bottom of the stairs and explain that the only food is what is on the table. Sit down with the rest of the family, leaving the fussy eater's food on the table, and try to ignore the child.

If the child changes her mind just as you're about to clear the table, then get the other members of the family to come back and wait until the fussy eater has finished.

Continue in this way with other meals. Don't be swayed if your child says she will eat her food watching TV or if she wants her dessert first. Explain that she must eat just like everyone else or go without.

If she begins to cry, sit her down in another room and return to the table. This is perhaps the hardest thing of all.

After a few days, there should be a glimmer of progress. Still offer tiny portions of food, followed by foods that you know your child will eat as a treat. Keeping to a plan like this is hard, but if the entire family sticks together and thinks positively, then it is possible. Keep to the time span you have decided, then suggest you all go to your local pizza or burger restaurant, and let the fussy eater choose what she likes.

**Fat Cat**

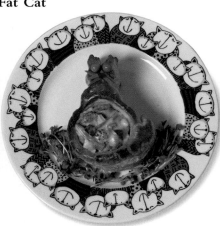

**Veggie Burger**

**Tuna Fish Cakes**

# LUNCH SPECIALS

Now that your baby has progressed from puréed to chopped food, you can begin to cook more grownup lunches. Try to introduce a range of different foods to give a balanced diet and a variety of tastes, but don't be disheartened if there are a few hiccups along the way.

## Sticky Chicken

**Serves 2–4**

4 chicken drumsticks

10ml/2 tsp oil

5ml/1 tsp soy sauce

15ml/1 tbsp smooth peanut butter

15ml/1 tbsp tomato ketchup

small baked potatoes, corn and tomato wedges, to serve

**1** Preheat the oven to 200°C/ 400°F/Gas 6 and line a small shallow baking tin (pan) with foil. Rinse the drumsticks under cold water, pat dry and peel off the skin. Make three or four slashes in the meat with a sharp knife and place in the tin.

**TIP**
If more convenient, use the peanut butter and ketchup mixture over chicken thighs or kebabs instead.

**2** Blend the remaining ingredients and spread thickly over the top of the chicken drumsticks. Cook in the oven for 15 minutes.

**3** Turn the drumsticks over and baste with the peanut butter mixture and meat juices.

**4** Cook for a further 20 minutes or until the juices run clear when the chicken is pierced with a knife.

**5** Cool slightly, then wrap a small piece of foil around the base of each drumstick. Arrange on plates and serve with small baked potatoes, hot corn, and tomato wedges.

# Coriander Chicken Casserole

**Serves 2**

2 chicken thighs

¼ small onion

1 small carrot, about 50g/2oz

50g/2oz swede (rutabaga)

5ml/1 tsp oil

2.5ml/½ tsp ground coriander

pinch of turmeric

5ml/1 tsp plain (all-purpose) flour

150ml/¼ pint/⅔ cup chicken stock

salt and pepper (optional)

mashed potatoes and peas, to serve

1 Preheat the oven to 180°C/ 350°F/Gas 4. Rinse the chicken under cold water, pat dry and trim away any excess skin if necessary. Chop the onion, carrot and swede.

2 Heat the oil in a frying pan, add the chicken and brown on each side. Add the vegetables.

**TIP**
Chop the meat for very young toddlers. Serve older children the whole thigh to make them feel more grown up, then help with cutting.

3 Stir in the coriander, turmeric and flour, then add the stock and a little salt and pepper, if liked. Bring to the boil, then transfer to a casserole.

4 Cover and cook in the oven for 1 hour. Spoon on to serving plates or into shallow dishes, cool slightly and serve the chicken casserole with mashed potatoes and peas.

# Chicken and Cheese Parcels

**Serves 2**

1 boned and skinned chicken breast, about 150g/5oz

25g/1oz Cheddar or mild cheese

1 slice lean ham, cut into 4 strips

15ml/1 tbsp oil

new potatoes, broccoli and carrots, to serve

1 Rinse the chicken under cold water, pat dry with kitchen paper and cut in half crossways. Place each half between two pieces of clear film (plastic wrap) and flatten with a rolling pin until each piece is about 10cm/4in square.

2 Cut the cheese in half and place a piece on each escalope (US scallop). Wrap the chicken around the cheese to enclose it completely.

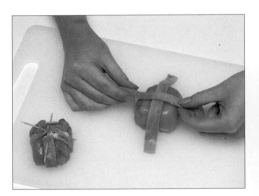

3 Arrange two pieces of the ham crossways over each of the parcels, securing them underneath with cocktail sticks (toothpicks). Brush the chicken parcels with oil.

**TIP**
You could wrap the parcels with halved rashers (strips) of rindless streaky (fatty) bacon, if preferred.

4 Place on a piece of foil and chill until ready to cook.

5 Preheat the grill (broiler). Cook the chicken for 10 minutes, turning once, until browned. Remove the cocktail sticks, cool slightly, then arrange on two plates and serve with new potatoes, steamed broccoli florets and sliced carrots.

# Peppered Beef Casserole

**Serves 2**

115g/4oz lean braising steak

¼ small onion

¼ small red (bell) pepper

¼ small yellow (bell) pepper

5ml/1 tsp oil

30ml/2 tbsp canned red kidney beans, drained and rinsed

5ml/1 tsp plain (all-purpose) flour

150ml/¼ pint/⅔ cup lamb stock

15ml/1 tbsp tomato ketchup

5ml/1 tsp Worcestershire sauce

45ml/3 tbsp couscous

a few drops of oil

40g/1½oz/3 tbsp frozen peas

salt and pepper (optional)

5 Bring to the boil, stirring, then transfer to a casserole dish, cover and cook in the oven for about 1½ hours, or until the meat is tender.

6 Just before serving place the couscous in a bowl, cover with boiling water and leave to soak for 5 minutes. Drain into a sieve (strainer) and stir in a few drops of oil.

7 Bring a pan of water to the boil, add the peas, and place the sieve of couscous over the pan. Cover and cook for 5 minutes.

8 Spoon the casserole on to two plates or dishes. Fluff up the couscous with a fork, drain the peas and spoon on to the plates. Cool slightly before serving.

1 Preheat the oven to 180°C/ 350°F/Gas 4. Rinse the meat under cold water and pat dry. Trim away any fat and cut into small cubes.

2 Chop the onion, remove the seeds and core from the peppers and cut into small cubes.

3 Heat the oil in a pan, add the beef and onion and fry gently until browned, stirring frequently.

4 Add the peppers and kidney beans, then stir in the flour, stock, tomato ketchup, Worcestershire sauce and a little salt and pepper if liked.

# Lamb Stew

**Serves 2**

115g/4oz lamb fillet

¼ small onion

1 small carrot, about 50g/2oz

½ small parsnip, about 50g/2oz

1 small potato

5ml/1 tsp oil

150ml/¼ pint/⅔ cup lamb stock

pinch of dried rosemary

salt and pepper (optional)

crusty bread, to serve

1 Rinse the lamb under cold water and pat dry. Cut away any fat from the meat and cut into small cubes. Finely chop the onion, then dice the carrot and parsnip and cut the potato into slightly larger pieces.

2 Heat the oil in a medium-size pan, add the lamb and onion, and fry gently until browned. Add the carrot, parsnip and potato, and fry the lamb and vegetables for a further 3 minutes, stirring.

3 Add the lamb stock, dried rosemary and a little salt and pepper, if liked. Bring to the boil, cover and simmer for 35–40 minutes, or until the meat is tender and moist.

4 Spoon the stew into shallow bowls and cool slightly before serving with crusty bread.

# Mexican Beef

**Serves 3–4**

¼ small onion

1 strip red (bell) pepper

½ small courgette (zucchini)

115g/4oz lean minced (ground) beef

1 small garlic clove, crushed

45ml/3 tbsp canned baked beans

45ml/3 tbsp beef stock

15ml/1 tbsp tomato ketchup

18 corn chips

25g/1oz/¼ cup grated Cheddar or mild cheese

green salad, to serve

1 Finely chop the onion and dice the pepper and courgette.

2 Dry fry the onion and meat in a medium-size pan, stirring until browned all over.

3 Stir in the remaining ingredients and bring to the boil, stirring. Cover and simmer the mixture for 15 minutes, stirring occasionally.

4 Place the corn chips on plates, spoon on the mixture and sprinkle the grated cheese over the top. Serve with a green salad.

# Lamb and Celery Casserole

**Serves 2**

115g/4oz lamb fillet

¼ onion

1 small carrot, about 50g/2oz

1 celery stick

25g/1oz button (white) mushrooms

5ml/1 tsp oil

bay leaf

10ml/2 tsp plain (all-purpose) flour

175ml/6fl oz/¾ cup lamb stock

salt and pepper (optional)

mashed potatoes and baby Brussels sprouts, to serve

1 Preheat the oven to 180°C/ 350°F/Gas 4. Rinse the lamb under cold water and pat dry, then trim off any fat and cut into small cubes. Chop the onion and carrot, rinse the celery and mushrooms, pat dry and slice thinly.

2 Heat the oil in a frying pan, add the lamb, onion and bay leaf and fry gently until the lamb is browned, stirring frequently. Add the remaining vegetables and fry for a further 3 minutes, until they are softened and lightly browned.

**VARIATION**
For a more unusual flavour, substitute fennel for the celery. Its slight aniseed taste goes well with lamb.

3 Stir in the flour, then add the stock, and a little salt and pepper, if liked. Bring to the boil and then transfer to a casserole, cover and cook in the oven for 45 minutes or until the meat is tender.

4 Spoon the casserole on to plates, discarding the bay leaf. Cool slightly, then serve with mashed potatoes and tiny Brussels sprouts.

# Shepherd's Pie

**Serves 2**

½ small onion

175g/6oz lean minced (ground)
  beef

10ml/2 tsp plain (all-purpose) flour

30ml/2 tbsp tomato ketchup

150ml/¼ pint/⅔ cup beef stock

pinch of mixed herbs

50g/2oz swede (rutabaga)

½ small parsnip, about 50g/2oz

1 medium potato, about 115g/4oz

10ml/2 tsp milk

15g/½oz/1 tbsp butter or margarine

½ carrot

40g/1½oz/3 tbsp frozen peas

salt and pepper (optional)

**1** Preheat oven to 190°C/375°F/
Gas 5. Finely chop the onion,
and place in a small pan with
the mince and dry fry over a low
heat, stirring, until the mince is
evenly browned.

**5** Spoon the meat into two
250ml/8fl oz/1 cup ovenproof
dishes. Place the mashed vegetables
on top, fluffing them up with a fork.
Dot with butter or margarine.

**6** Place both the pies on a baking
sheet and cook for 25–30 minutes,
until browned on top and bubbly.

**7** Peel and thinly slice the carrot
lengthways. Stamp out shapes
with petits fours cutters. Cook in a
pan of boiling water with the peas for
5 minutes. Drain and serve with the
shepherd's pies. Remember that baked
pies are very hot when they come out
of the oven. Always allow to cool
slightly before serving to children.

**2** Add the flour, stirring, then add
the ketchup, stock, mixed herbs
and seasoning, if liked. Bring to the
boil, cover and simmer gently for
30 minutes, stirring occasionally.

**3** Meanwhile, chop the swede,
parsnip and potato, and cook for
20 minutes, until tender. Drain.

**4** Mash with the milk and half of
the butter or margarine.

# Tuna Fish Cakes

**Serves 2–3**

| |
|---|
| 1 large potato, about 225g/8oz |
| knob (pat) of butter or margarine |
| 10ml/2 tsp milk |
| 5ml/1 tsp lemon juice |
| 100g/3½oz can tuna fish |
| 40g/1½oz/3 tbsp frozen corn, defrosted |
| flour, for dusting |
| 1 egg |
| 60ml/4 tbsp ground almonds |
| 50g/2oz green beans |
| ½ carrot |
| 6 frozen peas |
| 15ml/1 tbsp oil |
| salt and pepper (optional) |

**1** Peel and cut the potato into chunks and then cook in a pan of boiling water for about 15 minutes until tender. Drain and mash with the butter or margarine and milk.

**2** Add the lemon juice and a little salt and pepper, if liked. Drain the tuna fish and stir into the potato with the defrosted corn.

**3** Divide the mixture into six and pat each portion into a fish shape with floured hands.

**4** Beat the egg in a dish and place the ground almonds on a plate. Dip the fish cakes into the egg and then into the almonds, making sure they are completely covered. Place on a floured plate and chill until ready to cook.

**5** Trim the beans, and peel and cut the carrot into sticks a little smaller than the beans. Cook in a pan of boiling water with the peas for about 5 minutes.

**6** Meanwhile heat the oil in a frying pan, and fry the fish cakes for 5 minutes, until golden brown and crisp, turning once.

**7** Drain and arrange on serving plates with pea "eyes" and bean and carrot "pond weed". Cool slightly before serving.

# Fish and Cheese Pies

**Serves 2**

1 medium potato, about 150g/5oz

25g/1oz green cabbage

115g/4oz cod or hoki fillets

25g/1oz/2 tbsp frozen corn

150ml/¼ pint/⅔ cup milk

15ml/1 tbsp butter or margarine

15ml/1 tbsp plain (all-purpose) flour

25g/1oz/¼ cup grated Red Leicester
  or mild cheese

5ml/1 tsp sesame seeds

carrots and mangetouts (snowpeas),
  to serve

4 Strain the fish and corn, reserving the cooking liquid. Wash the pan, then melt the butter or margarine in the pan. Stir in the flour, then gradually add the reserved cooking liquid and bring to the boil, stirring until thickened and smooth.

5 Add the fish and corn with half of the grated cheese. Spoon into two small ovenproof dishes.

6 Mash the potato and cabbage with the remaining 10ml/2 tsp milk. Stir in half of the remaining cheese and spoon the mixture over the fish. Sprinkle with the sesame seeds and the remaining cheese.

7 Cook under a preheated grill until the topping is browned. Cool slightly before serving with carrot and mangetout vegetable fishes.

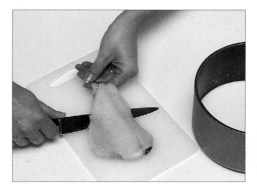

1 Peel and cut the potato into chunks and shred the cabbage. Cut any skin away from the fish fillets and rinse under cold water.

2 Bring a pan of water to the boil, add the potato and cook for 10 minutes. Add the cabbage and cook for a further 5 minutes until tender. Drain.

3 Meanwhile, place the fish fillets, the corn and all but 10ml/2 tsp of the milk in a second pan. Bring to the boil, then cover the pan and simmer very gently for 8–10 minutes, until the fish flakes easily when pressed with a knife.

# Surprise Fish Parcels

**Serves 2**

½ small courgette (zucchini)

175g/6oz smoked haddock or cod

1 small tomato

knob (pat) of butter or margarine

pinch of dried mixed herbs

new potatoes and broccoli, to serve

1 Preheat the oven to 200°C/ 400°F/Gas 6. Tear off two pieces of foil, then trim and thinly slice the courgette and divide equally between the two pieces of foil.

2 Cut the skin away from the fish, remove any bones, cut into two equal pieces and rinse under cold water. Pat the haddock dry and place on top of the courgettes.

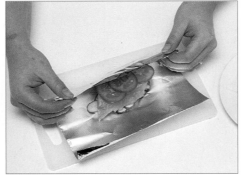

3 Slice the tomato and arrange slices on top of each piece of haddock. Add a little butter or margarine to each and sprinkle with mixed herbs.

4 Wrap the foil around the fish and seal the edges of each piece to make two parcels, then place the parcels on a baking sheet and cook in the oven for 15–20 minutes, depending on the thickness of the fish.

5 To test if they are cooked, open up one of the parcels and insert a knife into the centre. If the fish flakes easily, then it is ready.

6 Cool slightly, then arrange the parcels on plates and serve with new potatoes and broccoli.

# Cowboy Sausages and Beans

**Serves 2**

3 chipolata sausages

¼ small onion

1 small carrot, about 50g/2oz

1 strip red (bell) pepper

5ml/1 tsp oil

200g/7oz can baked beans

10ml/2 tsp Worcestershire sauce

fingers of toast, to serve

1 Press the centre of each sausage, twist and cut in half to make two small sausages.

2 Finely chop the onion, then dice the carrot and the pepper, discarding the core and seeds.

3 Heat the oil in a frying pan, add the sausages and the chopped onion and fry until browned.

**TIP**
Check the beans towards the end of cooking – you may need to add a little extra water.

4 Add the remaining ingredients and stir in 30ml/2 tbsp water. Cover and cook for 15 minutes, or until the carrot is cooked.

5 Spoon on to serving plates or into dishes, cool slightly and serve with fingers of toast.

# Mini Toad-in-the-Hole

**Serves 2**

3 chipolata sausages

5ml/1 tsp oil

60ml/4 tbsp plain (all-purpose) flour

1 egg

60ml/4 tbsp milk

salt

baked beans and green beans,
   to serve

1 Preheat the oven to 220°C/ 425°F/Gas 7. Press the centre of each sausage with your finger, twist and then cut in half. Brush two 10cm/4in tartlet tins (muffin pans) with oil. Add the sausages and cook for about 5 minutes.

2 Place the flour, egg and a pinch of salt in a bowl. Gradually whisk in the milk, beating until a smooth batter is formed.

3 Pour into the tins, quickly return to the oven and bake for 15 minutes, until risen and golden.

4 Loosen with a knife and turn out on to serving plates. Cool slightly and serve with baked beans and steamed green beans.

# Pork Hotpot

**Serves 2**

175g/6oz lean pork

¼ small onion

5ml/1 tsp oil

5ml/1 tsp plain (all-purpose) flour

40g/1½oz/3 tbsp frozen corn

pinch of dried sage

150ml/¼ pint/⅔ cup chicken stock

1 medium potato, about 150g/5oz

1 carrot, about 75g/3oz

knob (pat) of butter or margarine

salt and pepper (optional)

broccoli and Brussels sprouts,
  to serve

1 Preheat the oven to 180°C/
350°F/Gas 4. Rinse the pork
under cold water, pat dry, trim away
any fat and cut into small cubes. Peel
and finely chop the onion.

2 Heat the oil in a frying pan, add
the cubed pork and onion and
fry until golden brown, stirring.

3 Add in the flour and stir until
blended, then add the corn, dried
sage, stock and a little salt and pepper,
if liked. Bring to the boil and then
turn the mixture into a shallow
ovenproof dish.

4 Peel and thinly slice the potato
and carrot. Arrange slices so that
they overlap on top of the pork
mixture. Dot with butter or
margarine. Cover with foil and cook
in the oven for about 1 hour, until the
potatoes are tender.

5 Remove the foil and brown
under the grill (broiler) if liked.
Spoon on to serving plates, cool
slightly, then serve with steamed
broccoli and Brussels sprouts.

**TIP**

If you are cooking for only one
child, make the hotpot in two
dishes. Cool one, cover with clear
film (plastic wrap) and freeze for
up to three months.

# Pork and Lentil Casserole

**Serves 2**

175g/6oz boneless spare-rib pork chop

¼ small onion

1 small carrot, about 50g/2oz

5ml/1 tsp oil

1 small garlic clove, crushed

25g/1oz red lentils

90ml/6 tbsp canned chopped tomatoes

90ml/6 tbsp chicken stock

salt and pepper (optional)

swede (rutabaga) and peas, to serve

1 Preheat the oven to 180°C/ 350°F/Gas 4. Trim off any excess fat from the pork and cut in half. Finely chop the onion and dice the carrot.

2 Heat the oil in a frying pan, add the pork and onion and fry until the pork is browned on both sides.

3 Add the garlic, lentils and carrots and stir gently to mix.

4 Pour in the chopped tomatoes, stock and seasoning, if liked, and cook briefly to bring to the boil. Transfer to a casserole, cover and cook in the oven for 1¼ hours.

5 Spoon portions on to serving plates or shallow dishes and cool slightly. Serve with diced buttered swede and peas.

**TIP**

Teaching a child to use a knife and fork can be frustrating. Spare-rib pork chops are wonderfully tender when casseroled and so very easy to cut with a child's knife.

# Sticky Ribs and Apple Slaw

**Serves 2**

225g/8oz short pork ribs

10ml/2 tsp oil

10ml/2 tsp tomato ketchup

10ml/2 tsp hoisin sauce

1 medium potato, scrubbed but not peeled

knob (pat) of butter or margarine

*For the Apple Slaw*

½ carrot

½ eating apple

25g/1oz white cabbage

10ml/2 tsp sultanas (golden raisins)

30ml/2 tbsp mayonnaise

carrot slices, tomato wedges and celery sticks, to serve

1 Preheat the oven to 200°C/ 400°F/Gas 6. Rinse the pork ribs under cold water, pat dry and put on a roasting rack set over a small roasting pan. Mix the oil, ketchup and hoisin sauce, and brush over the ribs, reserving any extra mixture.

2 Pour a little boiling water into the base of the roasting pan. Prick the potato all over with a fork and then place in the oven with the spare ribs, preferably on the same shelf.

3 Cook for 1 hour, turning the pork ribs once during cooking and brushing with any of the remaining ketchup mixture.

4 Meanwhile peel the carrot, and peel, quarter and core the apple. Coarsely grate the apple and carrot and finely chop the cabbage.

5 Place in a bowl with the sultanas and mayonnaise and mix well.

6 Arrange the ribs on serving plates. Halve the baked potato, add a little butter or margarine to each half and serve with the pork ribs, together with star-shaped carrot slices, celery sticks and tomato wedges and spoonfuls of coleslaw.

**TIP**

Check the temperature of the ribs before serving, as they stay very hot for a surprisingly long time. Nothing will put a child off more than food that is very hot. Toddlers prefer their food to be lukewarm.

# Mini Cheese and Ham Tarts

**Makes 12**

*For the Pastry*

115g/4oz/1 cup plain (all-purpose) flour

50g/2oz/4 tbsp margarine

*For the Filling*

50g/2oz/½ cup mild cheese

2 thin slices ham, chopped

75g/3oz/½ cup frozen corn

1 egg

120ml/4fl oz/½ cup milk

pinch of paprika

salt and pepper

carrot and cucumber sticks, to serve

1 Preheat the oven to 200°C/400°F/ Gas 6. Place the flour in a bowl, add the margarine and rub in with your fingertips until the mixture resembles fine breadcrumbs.

2 Stir in 20ml/4 tsp water and mix to a smooth dough. Lightly knead and roll out on a floured surface.

3 Stamp out twelve 7.5cm/3in circles with a fluted cookie cutter, re-rolling the pastry as necessary. Press into a tartlet tin (muffin pan).

**TIP**
Encourage children to eat more vegetables by serving them with a yogurt dip flavoured with tomato purée (paste).

4 Grate the cheese, mix with the ham and corn, and divide among the pastry cases.

5 Beat together the egg, milk, salt and pepper and pour into the tarts. Sprinkle with paprika.

6 Cook in the oven for 12–15 minutes, until well risen and browned. Serve warm with carrot and cucumber sticks.

# GOING GREEN

GETTING CHILDREN TO EAT MORE THAN A FEW FROZEN PEAS AND THE ODD CARROT CAN BE AN UPHILL BATTLE. ENCOURAGE THEM TO BE A LITTLE MORE ADVENTUROUS BY MIXING THEIR FAVOURITE FOODS WITH SOME NEW VEGETABLES.

## Pick-up Sticks

**Serves 2**

5cm/2in piece of leek

25g/1oz green beans

1 strip red (bell) pepper

1 celery stick

25g/1oz beansprouts

1 small carrot, about 50g/2oz

5ml/1 tsp oil

15ml/1 tbsp tomato ketchup

5ml/1 tsp soy sauce

pinch ground ginger

grilled (broiled) sausages, to serve

1 Rinse the leek, beans, pepper, celery and beansprouts. Peel the carrot. Halve any large beans and beansprouts. Cut the remaining vegetables into thin strips.

2 Heat the oil in a frying pan, add all the vegetables except the beansprouts and fry for 3 minutes, stirring all the time.

3 Add the beansprouts, ketchup, soy sauce, ginger and 10ml/2 tsp water. Cook for a further 2 minutes, stirring until the vegetables are hot.

4 Spoon on to serving plates and leave to cool slightly. Serve with grilled sausages.

**TIP**

Don't overcook the vegetables. They should be quite crisp, and firm enough for your child to pick up.

# Spinach Pancakes with Ham and Cheese

**Serves 2–3**

50g/2oz fresh spinach, leaves only

50g/2oz plain (all-purpose) flour

1 egg yolk

300ml/½ pint/1¼ cups milk

15ml/1 tbsp oil

*For the Filling*

15ml/1 tbsp margarine

15ml/1 tbsp plain (all-purpose) flour

25g/1oz/¼ cup grated Red Leicester
   or mild cheese

40g/1½oz thinly sliced ham, chopped

40g/1½oz button (white) mushrooms,
   thinly sliced

1 Wash the spinach leaves well in cold water and then place in a frying pan, set over a medium heat. Cover and cook gently for 2–3 minutes, until the spinach has just wilted, stirring occasionally. Drain off any excess liquid and cool.

2 Put the flour, egg yolk and a little salt and pepper, if liked, into a bowl. Whisk in half of the milk to make a smooth batter. Finely chop the spinach and stir into the batter.

3 Melt the margarine in a pan, stir in the flour and then gradually stir in the remaining milk and bring to the boil, stirring continuously until smooth. Add the cheese, ham and mushrooms and stir to mix. Heat, cover and keep warm.

4 Heat a little oil in a frying pan, pour off excess, then add 30ml/ 2 tbsp pancake batter, tilting the pan so that the batter covers the base. Cook for a few minutes until browned, then flip over and cook the other side until golden. Slide the pancake on to a plate and keep warm.

5 Continue making pancakes until all the batter is used up.

6 Fold the pancakes into quarters, then spoon a little of the ham mixture into each one. Arrange the pancakes on plates and serve with tomato wedges and new potatoes.

**TIP**

If offering spinach to your child for the first time, make sure that the filling includes foods that you know are liked. Omit or add ingredients as necessary.

# Cauliflower and Broccoli with Cheese

**Serves 2**

1 egg

75g/3oz cauliflower

75g/3oz broccoli

15g/½oz/1 tbsp margarine

15ml/1 tbsp plain (all-purpose) flour

150ml/¼ pint/⅔ cup milk

40g/1½oz/⅓ cup grated Red
    Leicester or mild cheese

½ tomato

salt and pepper (optional)

1 Put the egg in a small pan of cold water, bring to the boil and cook for about 10 minutes until the egg is hard-boiled.

2 Meanwhile, cut the cauliflower and broccoli into florets and thinly slice the broccoli stalks. Cook in a pan of boiling water for about 8 minutes, until just tender.

3 Drain the vegetables and dry the pan. Melt the margarine, stir in the flour, then gradually mix in the milk and bring to the boil, stirring until thickened and smooth.

**TIP**
Making a face or fun pattern can be just enough to tempt a fussy eater to try something new.

4 Stir two-thirds of the cheese into the sauce together with a little seasoning, if liked. Reserve two of the broccoli florets and stir the remaining vegetables into the sauce.

5 Divide the mixture between two heat-resistant shallow dishes and sprinkle with the remaining cheese.

6 Place under a hot grill (broiler) until golden brown and bubbling.

7 Make a face on each dish with broccoli florets for a nose, a halved tomato for a mouth and peeled and sliced hard-boiled egg for eyes. Cool slightly before serving.

# Potato Boats

**Serves 2**

| |
|---|
| 2 small baking potatoes |
| 5cm/2in piece leek |
| 25g/1oz button (white) mushrooms |
| 10ml/2 tsp oil |
| 25g/1oz/2 tbsp frozen corn |
| 15ml/1 tbsp milk |
| knob (pat) of butter |
| ½ small courgette (zucchini), grated |
| 1 carrot, about 50g/2oz, grated |
| 2 slices processed cheese |
| 1 slice ham |
| salt and pepper (optional) |

1 Preheat the oven to 200°C/ 400°F/Gas 6. Prick the potatoes with a fork and bake for 1 hour, until soft. Alternatively, prick well and then microwave on a sheet of kitchen paper on High (full power) for 7–8 minutes.

2 Halve the leek lengthways, wash thoroughly to remove any grit and then slice thinly. Rinse the mushrooms, pat dry and thinly slice.

3 Heat 5ml/1 tsp oil in a frying pan and gently fry the leek, mushrooms and corn for about 3 minutes, until softened, stirring frequently. Turn into a bowl and keep warm.

4 When the potatoes are cooked, cut in half and scoop the centres into the bowl with the leek and mushroom mixture. Add the milk, butter and a little salt and pepper if liked, and stir to mix. Pile the mixture back into the potato shells.

5 Reheat the remaining 5ml/1 tsp of oil and fry the grated courgette and carrot for 2 minutes, until softened. Spoon on to two small plates and spread with a fork to cover the bases of the plates.

6 Arrange two potato halves on each plate. For sails, cut the cheese and ham into triangles and secure to potatoes with cocktail sticks. Cool slightly before serving.

# Fat Cats

**Serves 2**

oil, for greasing

200g/7oz frozen puff pastry, defrosted

a little flour, for dusting

beaten egg, to glaze

50g/2oz broccoli

25g/1oz/2 tbsp frozen mixed vegetables

15ml/1 tbsp butter or margarine

15ml/1 tbsp plain (all-purpose) flour

100ml/3½fl oz/½ cup milk

30ml/2 tbsp grated Cheddar or mild cheese

a little mustard and cress (fine curled cress), to garnish

1 Preheat the oven to 220°C/ 425°F/Gas 7 and lightly brush a baking sheet with a little oil. Roll out the pastry thinly on a surface lightly dusted with a little flour.

2 Using a shaped cookie cutter, stamp out four 13cm/5in cat shapes. Place two cats on the baking sheet and brush with egg.

3 Cut a large hole in the centres of the two remaining cats and place the shapes on top of the other two cats.

**VARIATION**
Ring the changes by making this recipe using different shaped cookie cutters for the pastry shapes. Get your child to choose his favourite.

4 Brush the tops with egg and cook for 10 minutes, until the pastry is well risen and golden.

5 Meanwhile chop the broccoli and cook in a small pan of boiling water with the frozen vegetables for 5 minutes. Drain.

6 Dry the pan and melt the butter or margarine. Stir in the flour and then gradually add the milk. Bring to the boil, stirring all the time until thickened and smooth.

7 Reserve two peas, two pieces of carrot, and two pieces of red bell pepper. Stir the remaining vegetables into the sauce with the grated cheese.

8 Enlarge the cavity in the centre of each pastry cat by scooping out a little of the pastry. Spoon in the vegetable mixture and arrange on two serving plates. Garnish with halved peas for eyes, halved carrot strips for whiskers and red pepper noses. Add mustard and cress. Cool slightly before serving.

# Potato, Carrot and Courgette Rösti

**Serves 2–4**

1 small potato, about 115g/4oz

½ carrot, about 25g/1oz

½ courgette (zucchini), about 25g/1oz

10ml/2 tsp vegetable oil

sausages and baked beans, to serve

1 Grate the potato, carrot and courgette into a bowl and mix together thoroughly.

2 Place several sheets of kitchen paper on a surface and put the vegetables on top. Cover with more kitchen paper and press down to soak up all the excess liquid.

3 Heat the oil in a frying pan and spoon the vegetables into the pan to form eight rounds. Flatten slightly with a fork and fry four of the rounds for 5 minutes, turning once until the potatoes are thoroughly cooked and the rösti is golden brown on both sides.

4 Lift out of the pan and cook the remaining mixture. Cool slightly and serve with grilled sausages and baked beans.

# Veggie Burgers

**Serves 2–4**

1 large or 2 small potatoes, about 225g/8oz

1 carrot, about 50g/2oz

25g/1oz broccoli

25g/1oz Brussels sprouts

1 egg yolk

15ml/1 tbsp plain (all-purpose) flour

15ml/1 tbsp freshly grated Parmesan cheese

15ml/1 tbsp oil

salt and pepper (optional)

canned spaghetti hoops, strips of ham, wedges of cucumber, and tomato ketchup, to serve

1 Cut the potato and carrot into chunks and cook in boiling water for 15 minutes, until tender.

2 Meanwhile, cut the broccoli into small florets, chop the stem finely and thinly slice the Brussels sprouts. Rinse under cold water then add to the potatoes and carrots for the last 5 minutes of cooking.

3 Drain the vegetables thoroughly and then mash together. Add the egg yolk, and a little salt and pepper, if liked, then mix well.

4 Divide into four and shape into burgers with floured hands. Coat in flour and Parmesan cheese.

5 Heat the oil in a frying pan, add the burgers and fry for 5 minutes, turning once until golden brown. Cool slightly, then serve with canned spaghetti hoops, strips of ham, a few cucumber wedges and a little tomato ketchup. Add a face with peas, carrot and cucumber.

**TIP**

To make a spider, add cooked green bean legs, a red (bell) pepper mouth and yellow pepper eyes.

# Vegetable Lasagne

**Serves 2–3**

¼ small onion

50g/2oz carrot

50g/2oz courgette (zucchini)

50g/2oz aubergine (eggplant)

25g/1oz button (white) mushrooms

10ml/2 tsp oil

1 small garlic clove, crushed

225g/8oz can chopped tomatoes

pinch of mixed herbs

15ml/1 tbsp butter or margarine

15ml/1 tbsp plain (all-purpose) flour

150ml/¼ pint/⅔ cup milk

60ml/4 tbsp grated mild cheese

3 sheets pre-cooked lasagne

salt and pepper

mixed salad, to serve

1 Finely chop the onion and carrot, and finely dice the courgette and aubergine. Wipe and thinly slice the mushrooms.

2 Heat the oil and fry the vegetables for 3 minutes until softened. Add the garlic, tomatoes and herbs, then bring to the boil, cover and simmer for 5 minutes.

3 Melt the butter or margarine in a pan, stir in the flour. Add the milk and bring to the boil, stirring, until thickened. Stir in half of the grated cheese and a little salt and pepper.

4 Preheat the oven to 180°C/ 350°F/Gas 4. Spoon one-third of the vegetable mixture into the base of an ovenproof dish, then add a little sauce. Add a slice of lasagne, then cover with half of the remaining vegetable mixture and half the remaining sauce.

5 Add a second sheet of pasta and top with the remaining vegetable mixture. Add a third sheet of lasagne and top with the remaining cheese sauce. Sprinkle with the remaining cheese.

6 Cook for 50–60 minutes, checking after 30 minutes and covering loosely with foil if the topping is browning too quickly. Spoon on to serving plates and leave the lasagne to cool slightly. Serve with a little mixed salad.

# Aubergine Bolognese

**Serves 2**

50g/2oz aubergine (eggplant)

1 strip red (bell) pepper

1 strip yellow (bell) pepper

5cm/2in piece of leek

1 carrot, about 50g/2oz

10ml/2 tsp oil

1 small garlic clove, crushed

25g/1oz/2 tbsp frozen corn

25g/1oz/2 tbsp red lentils

225g/8oz can chopped tomatoes

250ml/8fl oz/1 cup vegetable stock

pinch of dried herbs

50g/2oz dried pasta shapes

knob (pat) of butter or margarine

30ml/2 tbsp grated cheese (optional)

salt and pepper

1 Rinse the aubergine, peppers and leek, peel the carrot and then finely dice all the vegetables.

2 Heat the oil in a medium-size pan, add the diced vegetables and gently fry for 3 minutes, stirring frequently, until slightly softened.

**TIP**
Sprinkle the diced aubergine with salt, leave to drain in a colander for 30 minutes, then rinse. This removes any bitter taste.

3 Add the garlic, corn, lentils, tomatoes, stock, herbs and a little salt and pepper.

4 Bring to the boil, cover and simmer for about 30 minutes, stirring occasionally and adding a little extra stock if necessary.

5 In the last 10 minutes of cooking, bring a pan of water to the boil and add the pasta. Cook for 10 minutes, until tender.

6 Drain, toss in a little butter or margarine. Spoon on to plates and top with the aubergine bolognese. Sprinkle with cheese.

# QUICK MEALS

IF YOU'VE HAD A BUSY DAY, RUSTLE UP THESE QUICK AND TASTY TODDLERS' MEALS – THEY ALL COOK IN 10 MINUTES OR LESS, AND THERE IS A WIDE VARIETY OF RECIPES TO CHOOSE FROM. REMEMBER THE IMPORTANCE OF FUN PRESENTATION, TO TEMPT YOUR TODDLER TO TRY NEW FOODS.

## Speedy Chicken Pie

**Serves 2**

1 celery stick

25g/1oz/2 tbsp frozen corn, defrosted

30ml/2 tbsp mayonnaise

2.5ml/½ tsp ground coriander

75g/3oz cold cooked chicken

½ small packet plain crisps (US potato chips)

15ml/1 tbsp grated Red Leicester or mild cheese

salt and pepper (optional)

peas and broccoli, to serve

2 Spoon into a shallow ovenproof dish and level the surface.

3 Roughly crush the crisps and sprinkle over the chicken. Top with the grated cheese and cook for 10 minutes, until hot and bubbly.

4 Cool slightly, then serve the pie with peas and broccoli.

1 Preheat the oven to 220°C/425°F/ Gas 7. Rinse the celery, slice thinly and place in a bowl with the corn, mayonnaise, ground coriander and a little salt and pepper, if liked. Dice the chicken, add to the bowl and mix well.

**VARIATION**
**Mexican Chicken Pie**
Replace the ground coriander with ground cumin and replace the crisps with about 30ml/2 tbsp crumbled plain tortilla chips.

# Skinny Dippers

**Serves 2**

150g/5oz boneless, skinless chicken breast

25g/1oz/¼ cup grated Cheddar or mild cheese

50g/2oz/1 cup fresh breadcrumbs

15g/½oz/1 tbsp butter or margarine

115g/4oz frozen oven chips (french fries)

½ small carrot, cut into thin strips

½ small courgette (zucchini), cut into thin strips

45ml/3 tbsp tomato ketchup

1 Rinse the chicken under cold water and pat dry with kitchen paper. Cut into thin strips.

2 Mix the grated cheese and breadcrumbs on a plate. Melt the butter or margarine in a small pan or in a dish in the microwave on High (full power) for 20 seconds, then toss the chicken strips in the butter or margarine and roll in the breadcrumb mixture.

3 Arrange the chicken and chips on a foiled-lined baking sheet. Preheat the grill (broiler) and bring a pan of water to the boil.

4 Grill the chicken for 6–8 minutes and the chips 8–10 minutes, until both are well browned, turning once. When the chicken is ready, keep warm in a shallow dish while the chips finish cooking.

5 Cook the vegetables for 5 minutes in the pan of boiling water, until tender.

6 Spoon the ketchup into two ramekins or egg cups and place in the centre of two serving plates. Drain the vegetables and divide the vegetables, chicken and chips between the two plates. Allow to cool slightly before dipping into ketchup.

**TIP**

Keep a supply of fresh breadcrumbs in a sealed plastic bag in the freezer. There is no need to defrost, just take out as much as you need and use from frozen.

# Sweet and Sour Chicken

**Serves 2**

50g/2oz/¼ cup long grain white rice

1 carrot, about 50g/2oz

1 courgette (zucchini), about 50g/2oz

2 skinless chicken thighs

10ml/2 tsp oil

25g/1oz/2 tbsp frozen peas

5ml/1 tsp cornflour (cornstarch)

5ml/1 tsp soy sauce

10ml/2 tsp tomato ketchup

60ml/4 tbsp orange juice

1 egg, beaten

1 Cook the rice in boiling water for 8–10 minutes, until tender.

2 Meanwhile, peel the carrot, trim the courgette and cut both into thin strips. Bone the chicken and cut into small chunks.

3 Heat 5ml/1 tsp of the oil in a frying pan, add the carrot, courgette, chicken and peas, and fry for 5 minutes, stirring occasionally.

4 Blend the cornflour with the soy sauce and then stir into the pan together with the ketchup and orange juice. Cook gently, stirring all the time, until the sauce is glossy and has thickened.

**TIP**

Make the meal into an occasion and serve the food in Chinese bowls with Chinese spoons – chopsticks may be a little too tricky to manage. All children love the idea of eating in a restaurant with a parent to wait on them.

5 Drain the rice thoroughly. Add the remaining oil to the rice together with the beaten egg and cook over a gentle heat, stirring until the egg has scrambled.

6 Spoon the rice and sweet and sour chicken on to serving plates and cool slightly before serving.

# Ham and Tomato Scramble

**Serves 2**

| |
|---|
| 2 slices ham |
| 1 tomato |
| 1 small strip yellow (bell) pepper |
| 2 eggs |
| 15ml/1 tbsp milk |
| 2 slices bread |
| a little butter |
| salt |

1 Finely chop the ham. Halve the tomato, scoop out and discard the seeds, then chop into small dice. Finely chop the strip of pepper.

2 Beat the eggs and milk together and season with a little salt. Toast the bread lightly.

3 Heat a small knob (pat) of butter in a pan, add the eggs, ham, tomato and pepper and cook gently, stirring all the time until cooked to taste. Cool slightly.

4 Butter the toast and cut into shapes with small fancy-shaped cookie cutters. Arrange on plates with the ham and tomato scramble.

**TIP**
If you don't have any special cutters, then cut the toast into tiny triangles and squares with a knife.

# Ham Salad Clown

**Serves 2**

| |
|---|
| 2 slices ham |
| 1 cherry tomato |
| 2 slices apple |
| 1 slice cheese |
| 2 currants (raisins) |
| 2 slices hard-boiled egg |
| a little mustard and cress (fine curled cress) |
| 2 long slices carrot |

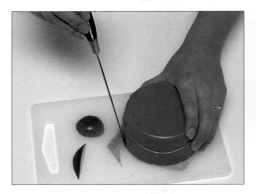

**TIP**
Have fun varying the ingredients for the clown. Use cheese slices, radishes, peaches, lettuce and red (bell) pepper to change the appearance and features.

1 Cut two large rounds from the slices of ham using a cookie cutter or the top of a glass or other container as a guide. Arrange on two plates and add a halved tomato for a nose and a slice of apple for the mouth, trimming if needed.

2 With a knife, cut out small triangles or stars of cheese for eyes, place on the ham and add halved currants (raisins) for eye balls.

3 Halve the egg slices and add to the face for ears. Snip the mustard and cress for hair and use snipped pieces of carrot for a ruff.

# Spanish Omelette

**Serves 2**

2 thin slices ham

1 strip red (bell) pepper

15ml/1 tbsp frozen peas

50g/2oz frozen oven chips (french fries)

5ml/1 tsp oil

1 egg

salt and pepper

tomato wedges, to serve

1 Chop the ham and pepper. Mix the pepper and peas. Slice the oven chips.

2 Heat the oil in a non-stick frying pan, and fry the chips for 5 minutes, stirring, until lightly browned. Add the pepper and peas and cook, stirring, for a further 2 minutes. Stir in the chopped ham.

3 Beat together the egg, 10ml/2 tsp water and a little salt and pepper, and pour into the pan, tilting it so that the egg mixture covers the base evenly.

4 Cook over a medium-low heat for 2–3 minutes, until the base of the omelette is set and browned. Loosen the edges and invert the pan on to a plate to turn out the omelette. Then slide the omelette back into the pan and cook the second side for a few more minutes, until golden.

5 Cut the omelette into wedges, arrange on two plates and cool slightly. Serve with tomato wedges.

# Pasta with Ham Sauce

**Serves 2**

50g/2oz dried pasta shapes

50g/2oz/½ cup frozen mixed vegetables

30ml/2 tbsp margarine

30ml/2 tbsp plain (all-purpose) flour

150ml/¼ pint/⅔ cup milk

50g/2oz/½ cup grated Red Leicester or mild cheese

2 slices ham, chopped

salt and pepper

1 Cook the pasta in a pan of boiling water for 5 minutes. Add vegetables and cook for 5 more minutes until pasta is tender. Drain.

2 Melt the margarine in a medium-size pan and stir in the flour. Gradually add the milk and bring to the boil, stirring, until the sauce is thick and smooth.

3 Stir two-thirds of the grated cheese into the sauce and add the drained pasta and vegetables, the ham and a little salt and pepper.

4 Spoon into two shallow dishes and sprinkle with the remaining cheese. Cool slightly if necessary.

**TIP**

This recipe works equally well if you use a 100g/3½oz can tuna, drained, in place of the ham. You could serve the ham with rice, if you prefer.

# Quickie Kebabs

**Serves 2–3**

| |
|---|
| 1 tomato |
| 3 slices ham |
| ½ small yellow (bell) pepper |
| 6 button (white) mushrooms |
| 6 cocktail sausages |
| 10ml/2 tsp tomato ketchup |
| 10ml/2 tsp oil |
| canned spaghetti, to serve |

1 Preheat the grill (broiler). Cut the tomato into six wedges and cut each slice of ham into two strips. Roll up each strip. Cut the pepper into six chunks, discarding any seeds. Wipe the mushrooms.

2 Make six kebabs by threading a tomato wedge, a ham roll, a piece of pepper, a mushroom, and a sausage on to six cocktail sticks (toothpicks).

**TIP**

Use two rashers (strips) of rindless bacon, if preferred. Halve and roll up, and use in place of the ham.

3 Line a grill pan with foil and arrange the kebabs on top. Blend the ketchup and oil, and brush over the kebabs. Grill for 10 minutes, turning once and brushing with the juices until the vegetables are browned and the sausages are thoroughly cooked.

4 Cool slightly, then arrange on plates with canned spaghetti.

# Sausage Wrappers

**Serves 2**

| |
|---|
| 4 slices ham |
| 10ml/2 tsp tomato relish or barbecue sauce |
| 4 sausages |
| baked beans and grilled potato shapes, to serve |

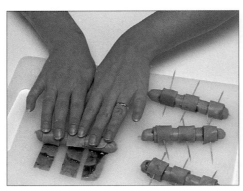

1 Spread one side of each slice of ham with relish or sauce.

2 Cut each piece of ham into three thin strips and wrap each sausage in three strips, securing them in place with cocktail sticks (toothpicks).

3 Grill (broil) for 10 minutes, turning several times until the ham is browned and crisp.

4 Cool slightly then remove the cocktail sticks and serve the sausage wrappers with baked beans and grilled potato shapes.

**TIP**

Use four pieces of rindless streaky (fatty) bacon instead of ham, if preferred.

# Corned Beef Hash

**Serves 2**

| |
| --- |
| 1 potato, about 175g/6oz |
| 10ml/2 tsp oil |
| 50g/2oz green cabbage |
| 115g/4oz corned beef |
| pinch of turmeric |
| 15ml/1 tbsp tomato ketchup |
| hard-boiled egg slices, to garnish |

1 Dice the potato and cook in a pan of boiling water for 3–4 minutes, until softened. Drain.

2 Heat the oil in a medium-size frying pan, add the diced potato and fry for 3 minutes, until golden.

3 Meanwhile, chop the cabbage and dice the corned beef.

4 Add the cabbage and turmeric to the pan with the potatoes and cook for 2 minutes. Stir in the corned beef and cook for 2 minutes.

5 Stir in the ketchup and spoon on to two plates. Cool slightly before serving. Garnish with the hard-boiled egg slices.

**TIP**

The hash can be garnished with tomato wedges, if liked.

# Cannibal Necklaces

**Serves 2**

45ml/3 tbsp stuffing mix

60ml/4 tbsp boiling water

115g/4oz lean minced (ground) beef

5ml/1 tsp oil

½ carrot

1 strip red (bell) pepper

1 strip green (bell) pepper

a little tomato ketchup

1 Put the stuffing mix in a bowl and pour over the boiling water. Set aside for 5 minutes to soak.

2 Stir the meat into the stuffing mix and shape into 10 small balls with floured hands.

3 Preheat the grill (broiler). Arrange the meat balls on a piece of foil on top of the grill pan and brush lightly with a little oil. Grill (broil) for 7–8 minutes, until well browned, turning once during cooking.

4 Meanwhile, thinly slice the carrot and cut the pepper into chunks, discarding the core and seeds.

5 Arrange the meat balls around the bottom edge of two serving plates. Leave spaces in between.

**TIP**

If you're feeling adventurous, liven up simple meals by piping the child's initials on to the edge of the plate, the appropriate number for their age or even a short word like "hello".

6 Place carrot and pieces of red and green pepper between each meat ball and complete with a line and bow of ketchup for necklace strings, straight from the bottle, or pipe the ketchup if preferred.

# Beef Burgers

**Serves 2**

¼ small onion

25g/1oz button (white) mushrooms

115g/4oz lean minced (ground) beef

115g/4oz frozen oven chips (french fries)

2 burger buns

10ml/2 tsp tomato ketchup

1 tomato

salt and pepper (optional)

**1** Finely chop the onion, wipe and chop the mushrooms. Place the meat in a mixing bowl, add the onion and mushrooms and a little salt and pepper, if liked, and mix together thoroughly. Alternatively blend the mixture in a processor.

**2** With floured hands shape two 7.5cm/3in burgers or press the mixture into a plastic burger press or upturned pastry cutter.

**3** Preheat the grill (broiler). Tear off two large pieces of foil. Fold up the edges and place on a grill pan. Put the burgers on one piece and the chips on the other.

**4** Cook the burgers and chips for 10 minutes, turning the food once. Remove from the grill rack and keep warm. Split the burger buns in half and toast on one side only.

**5** Spread the bases of the buns with ketchup, slice the tomato and place on the buns. Top each with a burger and the second bun half. Cut in half and arrange on serving plates with the chips. Cool slightly if necessary before serving.

# Four Fast Fishes

**Serves 2**

| |
|---|
| 115g/4oz hoki or cod fillet |
| ½ egg, beaten |
| 60ml/4 tbsp fresh breadcrumbs |
| 10ml/2 tsp sesame seeds |
| 10ml/2 tsp oil |
| 15ml/1 tbsp frozen peas |
| 4 frozen corn kernels |
| 1 carrot |
| canned spaghetti rings, to serve |

1 Cut away and discard any skin from the fish and rinse. Pat dry and cut into four pieces.

2 Put the egg in a saucer and place the breadcrumbs and sesame seeds on a plate. Dip pieces of fish in egg and then in breadcrumb mixture to coat the fish.

3 Heat the oil in a frying pan, add the fish and fry for 4–5 minutes, turning once, until the fish pieces are golden brown and cooked.

4 Meanwhile cook the peas and corn in a pan of boiling water for 5 minutes. Cut the carrot into long thin slices and then cut out fin and tail shapes and tiny triangles for mouths.

5 Arrange the pieces of fish on two plates with the carrot decorations, corn for eyes and peas for bubbles. Serve with warmed canned spaghetti rings.

**TIP**

You can freeze the uncooked breaded portions to provide a quick meal at a later date when you are pushed for time. Freeze them on a tray and then wrap them well to prevent the odour tainting other food in the freezer.

# Tuna Risotto

**Serves 2**

5ml/1 tsp oil

¼ onion, finely chopped

50g/2oz long grain white rice

50g/2oz frozen mixed vegetables

1 small garlic clove, crushed

10ml/2 tsp tomato ketchup

100g/3½oz can tuna fish in water

salt and pepper (optional)

1 Heat the oil in a small pan and fry the chopped onion for about 3 minutes, until softened.

2 Add the rice, mixed vegetables, garlic, tomato ketchup and 250ml/8fl oz/1 cup water and a little salt and pepper, if liked.

**TIP**
If liked use cold leftover cooked chicken, lamb or beef in place of the tuna.

3 Bring to the boil and simmer uncovered for 10 minutes. Drain the tuna and add to the rice mixture, stirring to mix. Cook for 3–4 minutes, stirring occasionally, until the water has been absorbed by the rice and the rice is tender.

4 Spoon on to plates and cool slightly before serving.

# Fish Finger Log Cabins

**Serves 2**

4 frozen fish fingers (breaded fish sticks)

25g/1oz green cabbage

8 mangetouts (snow peas)

2 frozen peas

1 strip green (bell) pepper

1 strip red (bell) pepper

1 Grill (broil) the fish fingers for 10 minutes, turning once until golden. Meanwhile, finely shred the cabbage and cook in boiling water for 3 minutes. Add the mangetouts and peas and cook for a further 2 minutes. Drain well.

2 Arrange two fish fingers side by side on each plate. Trim the mangetouts and use them to make a roof, slightly overlapping the edges of the fish fingers.

**VARIATION**
**Sausage Log Cabin**
Use four grilled (broiled) cocktail chipolata sausages for each cabin. Make the roof from green beans and use shredded spinach for the grass.

3 Cut four windows from the green pepper and two doors from the red pepper and add to the log cabins, using peas as door handles. Arrange the shredded cabbage to look like grass.

## TOAST TOPPERS

A LL CHILDREN, EVEN THE FUSSIEST OF EATERS, LOVE BREAD AND TOAST, AND THERE IS NO QUICKER CONVENIENCE FOOD. RING THE CHANGES WITH THESE SUPER-SPEEDY SNACKS THAT WILL MAKE MEAL-TIMES FUN.

## Shape Sorters

**Serves 2**

4 slices bread

butter or margarine, for spreading

30ml/2 tbsp smooth peanut butter

50g/2oz/½ cup grated Cheddar or
  mild cheese

4 cherry tomatoes

3 slices cucumber

**VARIATION**
**Pizza Shape Sorters**
Spread the shapes with tomato
ketchup. Chop a tomato finely, and
sprinkle over the shapes, then add
some grated mild cheese. Grill (broil)
until bubbly and golden.

1 Toast the bread lightly on both
sides and remove crusts. Stamp
out shapes using square, star,
triangle and round cutters.

2 Spread the shapes with butter or
margarine and then peanut
butter. Place the shapes on a baking
sheet and sprinkle with cheese.

3 Grill (broil) until the cheese is
bubbly. Cool slightly, arrange on a
plate and serve with tomato wedges
and quartered cucumber slices.

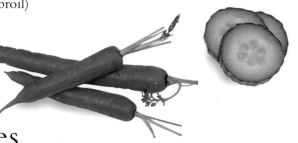

## Happy Families

**Serves 2**

3 slices bread

butter or margarine, for spreading

3 slices processed cheese

2 slices ham

a little mustard and cress (fine curled
  cress)

1 strip red (bell) pepper

½ carrot

small pieces of cucumber

1 Stamp out shapes of men and
women from the bread, using
small cutters. Spread with a little
butter or margarine.

2 Stamp out cheese dresses using
the woman cutter and trimming
off the head. Press on to three of the
bodies. Cut out cheese jumpers and
ham trousers and braces. Add to the
male shapes.

3 Snip off the leaves from mustard
and cress and use for eyes. Cut
tiny red pepper mouths and make
necklaces and bow ties from the
carrot and cucumber, using flower
cutters. Arrange on plates.

# French Toast Butterflies

**Serves 2**

| |
|---|
| 4 small broccoli florets |
| 8 peas |
| 1 small carrot |
| 1 slice Red Leicester or mild cheese |
| 2 slices ham |
| 2 slices bread |
| 1 egg |
| 10ml/2 tsp milk |
| 5ml/1 tsp vegetable oil |
| a little tomato ketchup |

1 Cook the broccoli florets and the peas in a pan of boiling water for 5 minutes. Drain well.

2 For each butterfly, cut four thin slices of carrot and cut into flower shapes with a petits four cutter. Cut out four small squares from the cheese.

3 Cut four thin strips from the rest of the carrot for antennae. Roll up each piece of ham and arrange in the middle of two serving plates, to make the two butterfly bodies.

4 Cut butterfly wings from the bread, using a small knife.

**TIP**
Vary the ingredients for the butterfly decorations. Make a body from a grilled sausage if preferred.

5 Beat together the egg and milk and dip the bread in to coat both sides thoroughly. Heat the oil in a medium-size frying pan and fry the bread until golden on both sides.

6 Assemble the butterfly, using the French toast for the wings and decorating with the carrot, cheese, broccoli and peas. Use a blob of ketchup for the head.

# Tuna Flowers

**Serves 2–3**

6 thin slices bread

25g/1oz butter, plus extra if
  necessary

10ml/2 tsp plain (all-purpose) flour

75ml/5 tbsp milk

60ml/4 tbsp grated Red Leicester or
  mild cheese

100g/3½oz can tuna fish, drained

50g/2oz/4 tbsp frozen mixed
  vegetables, defrosted

½ carrot

6 slices cucumber, halved

a little mustard and cress (fine curled
  cress)

salt and pepper (optional)

1 Preheat the oven to 200°C/
400°F/Gas 6. Cut out six flower
shapes from the bread, using a 9cm/
3½in scalloped cookie cutter. Flatten
each piece slightly with a rolling pin.

2 Melt the butter in a pan or
microwave. Brush a little over
one side of each piece of bread and
then press the bread, buttered side
downwards, into sections of a patty tin
(muffin pan). Brush the second side of
the bread with a little more butter.

3 Bake in the oven for about 10–
12 minutes, until crisp and
golden around the edges.

4 Stir the flour into the remaining
butter (you should have about
10ml/2 tsp left). Gradually stir in the
milk and bring to the boil, stirring
until the sauce is thick and smooth.

5 Stir in 30ml/3 tbsp of the cheese,
the tuna, the mixed vegetables
and a little salt and pepper, if liked.

6 Heat through and then spoon
into the baked bread cups and
sprinkle with remaining cheese.

7 Arrange the tuna cups on
serving plates. Cut the carrot
into thin strips for flower stems and
add to the plate, with halved
cucumber slices for leaves and
mustard and cress for grass.

# Noughts and Crosses

**Serves 2**

8 green beans

¼ red (bell) pepper

6 slices snack dried sausage

2 slices bread

butter or margarine, for spreading

115g/4oz Cheddar or mild cheese

**TIP**

To vary the topping, use thin strips of carrot or ham for the grid, sliced sausage, frankfurter or carrot for the noughts (zeros), carrot, green (bell) pepper or cucumber for the crosses. (The game of noughts and crosses is also known as tic-tac-toe in the USA.)

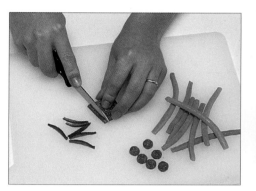

1 Trim the beans, thinly slice the pepper, discarding any seeds, and thinly slice the sausage.

2 Cook the beans in boiling water for 5 minutes. Toast the bread lightly on both sides and spread with butter or margarine. Thinly slice the cheese and place on the toast.

3 Drain the beans and arrange four on each piece of toast to form a grid. Add crosses made from pepper strips and noughts from pieces of the sausage.

4 Grill (broil) the toasts until the cheese is bubbly. Arrange on plates and cool slightly before serving.

# Cheese Strips on Toast

**Serves 2**

2 slices bread

butter or margarine, for spreading

50g/2oz Cheddar or mild yellow cheese

50g/2oz red Leicester or mild red cheese

2 cherry tomatoes, to serve

1 Toast the bread lightly on both sides, then spread each slice with butter or margarine.

**TIP**

If your child likes ketchup or peanut butter, add a thin scraping underneath the cheese slices for a surprise flavour.

2 Thinly slice the cheese and then cut into strips about 2.5cm/1in wide. Arrange alternate coloured cheese strips over the toast and grill (broil) the toasts until bubbly.

3 Cool slightly, then cut into squares, arrange on plates and serve with cherry tomato wedges.

# Speedy Sausage Rolls

**Makes 18**

8 slices multigrain white bread

225g/8oz cocktail sausages

40g/1½oz/3 tbsp butter or
  margarine

carrot and cucumber sticks, to serve

1 Preheat the oven to 190°C/
375°F/Gas 5. Trim the crusts off
the bread and cut into slices a little
smaller than the sausages.

2 Wrap each piece of bread around
a sausage and secure with a
halved cocktail stick (toothpick). Place
the sausage rolls on a baking sheet.

3 Melt the butter or margarine in a
small pan or in the microwave and
brush over the prepared sausage rolls.

4 Bake in the oven for 15 minutes,
until browned. Cool slightly
and remove the cocktail sticks.
Arrange on a plate and serve with
carrot and cucumber sticks.

**TIP**
Spread a little tomato relish or
ketchup, or a little mild mustard
over the bread before wrapping it
around the sausages, to give a
sharper flavour. If the bread is
thickly cut, flatten it slightly with a
rolling pin, before wrapping around
the sausages.

# Pizza Clock

**Serves 3–4**

20cm/8in ready-made pizza base

45ml/3 tbsp tomato ketchup or pizza sauce

2 tomatoes

75g/3oz/¾ cup grated mild cheese

pinch of dried marjoram

1 green (bell) pepper

1 large carrot

1 thick slice ham

**1** Preheat oven to 220°C/425°F/ Gas 7. Place the pizza base on a baking sheet and spread with ketchup or pizza sauce. Chop the tomatoes and scatter over the pizza with the cheese and marjoram.

**2** Place directly on an oven shelf and bake for 12 minutes, until the cheese is bubbly. (Place a baking tray on the shelf below the pizza to catch any drips of cheese.)

**3** Meanwhile halve the pepper, cut away the core and seeds and stamp out the numbers 3, 6, 9 and 12 with small number cutters. Peel and thinly cut the carrot lengthways and stamp out the numbers 1, 2, 4, 5, 7, 8, 10 and 11. Arrange on the pizza to form a clock face.

**4** Cut out a carrot circle. Cut two clock hands, each about 7.5cm/ 3in long from the ham. Arrange on the pizza with the circle of carrot.

**5** Place the pizza clock on to a serving plate and arrange the numbers around the edge. Cool the pizza clock slightly before cutting into wedges and serving.

**TIP**

If preferred, make a smaller version of this using half a toasted muffin. Top as above and grill (broil) until the cheese melts. Add ham hands and small pieces of carrot to mark the numbers.

# Spotted Sandwiches

**Serves 2**

| |
|---|
| 1 hard-boiled egg |
| 30ml/2 tbsp mayonnaise |
| 2 slices white bread |
| 2 slices brown bread |
| a little mustard and cress (fine curled cress) |
| ½ small carrot |

1 Peel and finely chop the egg, place in a small bowl and blend well with the mayonnaise.

2 Stamp out giraffe shapes from the brown and white bread, using an animal cookie cutter.

3 Cut tiny rounds from each shape, using the end of a metal piping tube, and then replace the rounds with opposite-coloured bread circles.

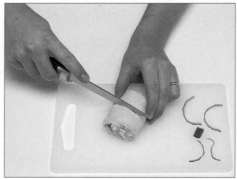

4 Spread the egg and mayonnaise over half of the shapes and top with the remaining shapes. Arrange on plates with snipped mustard and cress for grass and shaped carrot slices for flowers.

# Sandwich Snails

**Serves 2**

| |
|---|
| 1 strip red (bell) pepper |
| small piece cucumber |
| 15ml/1 tbsp frozen corn, defrosted |
| 25g/1oz/¼ cup grated Cheddar or mild cheese |
| 15ml/1 tbsp mayonnaise |
| 1 slice bread |
| 2 cooked sausages |
| a little shredded lettuce |

1 Cut away any seeds from the pepper and cut out four small squares for the snails' eyes. Cut four strips of cucumber for their antennae. Finely chop the remaining pepper and cucumber and mix with the corn, cheese and mayonnaise. Place in a bowl.

2 Trim the crusts off the bread, cut in half and overlap two short edges together to make a long strip. Flatten slightly with a rolling pin so that the bread bonds together.

**VARIATION**
For pasta snails, use large shell pasta instead of the bread, and stuff with the cheese mixture.

3 Spread the bread with the cheese mixture and roll up tightly. Squeeze together, then cut in half crossways to make two rounds.

4 Arrange each slice, cut side uppermost, on two serving plates. Arrange the sausages as bodies, and use the cucumber strips for antennae and the red pepper squares for the eyes. Arrange the shredded lettuce as grass.

# EASY DESSERTS

WITH A YOUNG FAMILY TO FEED, DESSERTS NEED TO BE QUICK, LIGHT AND TASTE GOOD WITHOUT THE KIDS REALIZING THAT THEY'RE HEALTHY TOO! REMEMBER TO KEEP SUGAR TO A MINIMUM.

## Fruit Fondue

**Serves 2**

150g/5oz tub ready-to-serve low-fat custard

25g/1oz milk chocolate

1 eating apple

1 banana

1 satsuma or clementine

a few strawberries or seedless grapes

**1** Pour the custard into a pan, add the chocolate and heat, stirring all the time until the chocolate has melted. Cool slightly.

**2** Quarter the apple, core and cut into bitesize pieces, slice the banana and break the satsuma or clementine into segments. Hull the strawberries and wash the grapes.

**3** Arrange the fruit on two small plates, pour the custard into two small dishes and place on the plates. The fruit can be dipped into the custard, using either a fork or fingers.

**TIP**

Add the chocolate to a tub of custard and microwave on Full Power (100%) for 1½ minutes, or until the chocolate has melted. Stir and spoon into dishes. Cool slightly.

# Apple and Orange Fool

**Makes: 250ml/8fl oz/1 cup**

2 eating apples

5ml/1 tsp grated orange rind and 15ml/1 tbsp orange juice

15ml/1 tbsp custard powder

5ml/1 tsp caster (superfine) sugar

150ml/¼ pint/⅔ cup formula milk

1 Quarter, core and peel the apples. Slice and place the apples in a pan with the orange rind and juice.

2 Cover and cook gently for 10 minutes, stirring occasionally until the apples are soft.

3 Blend the custard powder and sugar with a little of the milk to make a smooth paste. Bring the remaining milk to the boil and stir into the custard mixture.

4 Return the custard to the pan and slowly bring to the boil, stirring until thickened and smooth.

5 Process or mash the apple to the desired consistency. Add the custard and stir to mix.

6 Spoon a little into a bowl, test the temperature and cool if necessary before serving.

7 Cover the remaining fool and transfer to the refrigerator as soon as possible. Use within 24 hours.

• Suitable for freezing.

# Peach Melba Dessert

**Makes: 175ml/6fl oz/3/4 cup**

1 ripe peach

25g/1oz fresh or frozen raspberries

15ml/1 tbsp icing (confectioners') sugar

115g/4oz Greek (US strained plain)
   yogurt

1 Halve the peach, discard the
   stone (pit), then peel and slice.
Place in a pan with the raspberries and
15ml/1 tbsp water.

2 Cover and cook gently for
   10 minutes, until soft.

3 Purée and press through a sieve
   (strainer) to remove the raspberry
pips (seeds).

**TIP**

The finished dessert is not suitable
for freezing, but the sweetened
fruit purée can be frozen in
sections of an ice-cube tray. Defrost
cubes of purée and mix each cube
with 15ml/1 tbsp yogurt.

4 Set aside to cool, then stir in the
   sugar and swirl in the yogurt.
Spoon a little into a dish.

5 Cover the remaining dessert and
   transfer to the refrigerator. Use
within 24 hours.

**VARIATION**
**Bananarama**
To make a single portion, use ½
a small banana and 15ml/1 tbsp of
Greek (US strained plain) yogurt.
Mash the banana until smooth and
add the yogurt. Stir to mix and serve
immediately. Do not make this
dessert in advance, as the banana will
discolour while standing.

# Strawberry Ice Cream

**Makes 900ml/1½ pints/3¾ cups**

300ml/½pint/1¼ cups double (heavy) cream

425g/15oz can custard

450g/1lb strawberries

teddy bear wafers, to decorate

strawberries, to decorate

1 Whip the cream until softly peaking, then fold in the custard.

2 Hull the strawberries and then rinse and pat dry. Process to make a smooth purée, then press through a sieve (strainer) into the cream and custard. Fold together.

3 Pour the mixture into a plastic tub and freeze the ice cream for 6–7 hours, until half frozen.

4 Beat the ice cream with a fork or process in a food blender until smooth, then return the tub to the freezer and freeze until solid.

5 Remove the ice cream from the freezer 10 minutes before serving so that it can soften slightly. Scoop into serving bowls and decorate each with teddy bear wafers and extra fruit, such as strawberries.

## VARIATIONS
**Strawberry Ripple Ice Cream**
Purée and sieve (strain) an extra 250g/9oz strawberries and sweeten with 30ml/2 tbsp icing (confectioners') sugar. Swirl this into the half-frozen ice cream at Step 4 and then freeze until solid.

**Apricot and Chocolate Chip Ice Cream**
Whisk 300ml/½ pint/1¼ cups double (heavy) cream, and fold in 425g/15oz can custard. Drain and purée the contents of a 425g/15oz can apricot slices in natural juice and stir into the cream with the finely grated rind of 1 orange. Pour into a plastic tub, freeze until mushy and then beat well. Stir in 100g/3½oz packet chocolate dots and freeze again until solid. Scoop into serving dishes and decorate the ice cream with orange segments and wafers, if liked.

# Raspberry Sorbet

**Makes: 900ml/1½ pints/3¾ cups**

10ml/2 tsp powdered gelatine

600ml/1 pint/2½ cups water

225g/8oz/1¼ cups caster (superfine)
   sugar

675g/1½lb raspberries, hulled

grated rind and juice of ½ lemon

**1** Put 30ml/2 tbsp water in a cup, sprinkle the gelatine over and set aside for a few minutes to soak.

**2** Place the water and sugar in a pan and heat, stirring occasionally, until the sugar has completely dissolved.

**3** Bring to the boil and boil rapidly for 3 minutes. Remove from the heat, add the gelatine mixture to the syrup and stir until completely dissolved. Leave to cool.

**4** Liquidize or process the raspberries to a smooth purée, then press through a sieve (strainer) into the syrup. Stir in the lemon rind and juice.

**5** Pour into a plastic tub and freeze for 6–7 hours, or until the mixture is half frozen.

**6** Beat the sorbet with a fork or transfer to a food processor and process until smooth. Return to the freezer and freeze until solid.

**7** Remove the sorbet from the freezer 10 minutes before serving to soften slightly, then scoop into dishes with a melon baller or small teaspoon.

**VARIATION**
**Summer Fruit Sorbet**
Follow the recipe up to Step 3. Put a 500g/1¼lb pack of frozen summer fruits into a second pan. Add 60ml/4 tbsp water, cover and cook for 5 minutes until soft, then purée and sieve (strain), add to the syrup and continue as above.

# Yogurt Lollies

**Makes 6**

150g/5oz tub strawberry yogurt

150ml/¼ pint/⅔ cup milk

10ml/2 tsp strawberry milkshake
  powder

1 Mix the yogurt, milk and milkshake powder together.

2 Pour the mixture into six small lolly (popsicle) plastic moulds. Add the handles and freeze overnight.

**TIP**
Store lollies (popsicles) for up to a week in the freezer. Make sure they are tightly covered, as they can pick up other flavours.

3 Dip the moulds into hot water, count to 15, then flex handles and remove. Serve at once.

# Jolly Jellies

**Serves 4**

150g/5oz packet strawberry jelly
  (flavoured gelatine)

2 ripe plums

175g/6oz fromage frais or Greek
  (US strained plain) yogurt

4 dolly mixtures (round candies)

10ml/2 tsp sugar or chocolate strands

1 Cut the jelly into pieces. Place in a bowl and pour over 150ml/¼ pint/⅔ cup boiling water. Stir until dissolved, then set aside to cool.

2 Halve the plums, cut away the stones (pits) and reserve four thin slices. Chop the remaining fruit and divide among four small dishes.

**TIP**
If the fussy eater doesn't like different textures, finely chop or purée the plums before adding to the jelly (flavoured gelatine) so the child doesn't know it's not just jelly!

3 Stir the fromage frais or yogurt into the jelly and pour into the dishes. Chill in the refrigerator until set.

4 Decorate with sliced plums for mouths, halved dolly mixtures for the eyes and sugar or chocolate sugar strands for hair.

# Pancakes

**Serves 2–3**

| |
|---|
| 50g/2oz/⅓ cup plain (all-purpose) flour |
| 1 egg |
| 150ml/¼ pint/⅔ cup milk |
| 15ml/1 tbsp vegetable oil |
| *For the filling* |
| 1 banana |
| 1 orange |
| 2–3 scoops ice cream |

**1** Sift the flour into a bowl, add the egg and gradually whisk in the milk to form a smooth batter. Whisk in 5ml/1 tsp of the oil.

**2** To make the filling, slice the banana thinly or in chunks. Cut the peel away from the orange with a serrated knife, then cut the orange into segments.

**3** Heat a little of the remaining oil in a medium-size non-stick pan, pour off any excess oil and add 30ml/2 tbsp of the batter. Tilt the pan to evenly coat it and cook for a couple of minutes, until the pancake is set and the underside is golden.

**4** Loosen the edges with a knife, then toss the pancake or turn with a knife. Brown the other side and then slide out on to a plate. Fold in four and keep warm.

**5** Cook the rest of the batter in the same way until you have made 6 pancakes. Place two on each plate.

**6** Spoon a little fruit into each pancake and arrange on serving plates. Top with the remaining fruit and a scoop of ice cream, and pour over a little maple syrup. Serve at once.

# Traffic Light Sundaes

**Serves 6**

½ packet lime jelly (flavoured gelatine)

½ packet orange jelly

½ packet strawberry jelly

2 kiwi fruits

275g/10oz can mandarin oranges

6 scoops vanilla ice cream, to serve

12 strawberries to decorate

4 Add a little kiwi fruit and continue making layers using the orange jelly and mandarins and topping with the strawberry jelly.

5 Add half the strawberries, top with a scoop of ice cream and decorate with the remaining strawberries. Serve immediately.

1 Make up each jelly in a separate bowl with boiling water according to the instructions on the packet. Cool, then transfer to the refrigerator and allow to set.

2 Peel and slice the kiwi fruits, hull and rinse the strawberries and cut in half. Drain the mandarins.

3 Chop all of the jellies and divide the lime jelly equally among six sundae glasses.

**TIP**

This is a great recipe for a party – simple but ever popular. For smaller numbers of children, halve the recipe to make three. For tiny children, make up half-size sundaes in plastic cups.

# Cheat's Trifle

**Serves 2**

2 slices Swiss roll (jelly roll)

20ml/4 tsp orange juice

1 mandarin orange

50g/2oz strawberries

150g/5oz tub ready-to-serve custard

10ml/2 tsp Greek (US strained plain) yogurt

2 sugar flowers, to decorate

**TIP**
Use 150ml/¼ pint/⅔ cup leftover custard if you have it or make custard with custard powder and 150ml/¼ pint/⅔ cup milk.

1 Put a slice of Swiss roll in the base of two ramekin dishes and spoon the orange juice over the top. Peel the mandarin orange and divide the segments between the dishes.

2 Hull, rinse and chop the strawberries. Place in dishes.

3 Spoon the custard over the strawberries, top with yogurt and decorate with sugar flowers.

# Baked Bananas

**Serves 2**

2 medium bananas

2 small scoops ice cream

1 Preheat the oven to 180°C/ 350°F/Gas 4. Separate the unpeeled bananas and put on a baking sheet. Cook for 10 minutes, until the skins have blackened and the bananas feel quite soft.

2 Hold the banana in a dish towel, make a slit along the length of the banana and peel off the skin. Peel the second banana.

3 Slice and arrange each as a ring on a plate. Place a scoop of ice cream in the centre of each plate.

**TIP**
For an adult version, slit the banana and spoon in a teaspoon or two of coffee cream liqueur, eat out of the skin with a teaspoon.

# Quick Cakes and Bakes the Kids can Make

Cooking is fun, and the earlier you learn, the more fun it is. Even the faddiest eater can be an enthusiastic cook, and helping to decide what to cook for a meal can make a child more willing to sit down with the family and hand round their home-made goodies. Learning to weigh out ingredients, and to mix, spread and spoon out, all helps with co-ordination and encourages a basic interest in and love of food.

**Getting ready**
- Find a large apron or cover the child's clothes with an old adult-size shirt with the sleeves cut down.
- Always wash the child's hands before you start to cook.

- Choose a sturdy chair for your child to stand on next to the work surface or table. Alternatively, put a large cloth on the floor, set scales, bowls, ingredients etc out, and prepare food sitting down.

- Make it clear to your child that only the adult opens the oven door and touches pans on the stove.
- Keep knives and scissors out of the way; provide blunt, round-ended scissors if required.

## Orange and Apple Rockies

**Makes 24**

oil, for greasing

115g/4oz/½ cup margarine

225g/8oz/2 cups self-raising (self-rising) flour

1 large eating apple

50g/2oz ready-to-eat dried apricots

50g/2oz sultanas (golden raisins)

grated rind of 1 small orange

75g/3oz/⅓ cup demerara (raw) sugar

1 egg

15ml/1 tbsp milk

apple slices, to serve

1 Preheat the oven to 190°C/375°F/ Gas 5 and brush two baking sheets with a little oil. Rub the margarine into the flour with your fingertips until the mixture resembles fine breadcrumbs.

2 Peel, core and finely chop the apple, chop the apricots and stir into the flour mixture with the sultanas and orange rind. Reserve 30ml/2 tbsp of the sugar and stir the rest into the mixture.

3 Beat the egg and milk, add to the flour mixture and mix until just beginning to bind together.

4 Drop spoonfuls, well spaced apart, on to the baking sheet. Sprinkle with the reserved sugar and bake in the oven for 12–15 minutes. Transfer to a serving plate and serve warm or cold with apple slices.

**TIP**
Freeze any left-over rockies in a plastic bag for up to three months.

# Mini Cup Cakes

**Makes: 26**

50g/2oz/4 tbsp soft margarine

50g/2oz/¼ cup caster (superfine) sugar

50g/2oz/⅓ cup self-raising (self-rising) flour

1 egg

**1** Preheat the oven to 180°C/350°F/ Gas 4. Place 26 paper mini muffin cases on a large baking sheet.

**2** Put all the ingredients for the cake into a mixing bowl and beat together well until smooth.

**3** Divide the mixture among the cases and cook for 8–10 minutes, until well risen and golden.

**4** Transfer the cakes to a wire rack and leave to cool completely, then peel the paper off one or two cakes and serve.

**5** Store the remaining cakes in a plastic box for up to three days.

• Suitable for freezing up to three months in a plastic box.

**TIP**

Cut a cup cake in half crossways and spread one half with a little sugar-free jam. Replace top half and serve.

# Shortbread Shapes

**Makes: 60**

little oil, for greasing

150g/5oz/1 cup plain (all-purpose) flour

25g/1oz/3 tbsp cornflour (cornstarch)

50g/2oz/¼ cup caster (superfine) sugar

115g/4oz/½ cup butter

extra sugar, for sprinkling (optional)

**1** Preheat the oven to 180°C/ 350°F/Gas 4. Brush two baking sheets with a little oil.

**2** Put the flour, cornflour and sugar in a bowl. Cut the butter into pieces and rub into the flour until the mixture resembles fine breadcrumbs. Mould to a dough with your hands.

**3** Knead lightly and roll out on a floured surface to a 5mm/¼in thickness. Stamp out shapes with small cookie or petits fours cutters.

**4** Transfer to the baking sheets, sprinkle with extra sugar, if liked, and cook for 10–12 minutes, until pale golden. Loosen with a knife and leave to cool on the baking sheets, then transfer to a wire rack.

**5** Offer your child one or two shapes and store the rest in a plastic box for up to one week.

**TIP**

These biscuits (cookies) will keep well in the freezer for three months. Pack in rigid plastic boxes and thaw in a single layer. If you prefer, you can freeze them before baking. Wrap well to prevent them taking up flavours from other food.

# Date Crunch

**Makes 24 pieces**

225g/8oz packet digestive biscuits (graham crackers)

75g/3oz stoned (pitted) dates

75g/3oz/⅓ cup butter

30ml/2 tbsp golden (light corn) syrup

75g/3oz sultanas (golden raisins)

150g/5oz milk or dark (bittersweet) chocolate

**1** Line an 18cm/7in shallow baking tin (pan) with foil. Put the biscuits in a plastic bag and crush roughly with a rolling pin. Finely chop the dates.

**2** Gently heat the butter and syrup in a small pan until the butter has melted.

**TIP**

For an alternative topping, drizzle 75g/3oz melted white and 75g/3oz melted dark (bittersweet) chocolate over the biscuit, to make random squiggly lines. Chill until set.

**3** Stir in the crushed biscuits, the dates and sultanas and mix well. Spoon into the tin, press flat with the back of a spoon and chill for 1 hour.

**4** Break the chocolate into a bowl, melt over hot water, and then spoon over the biscuit mixture, spreading evenly with a palette knife. Chill until set.

**5** Lift the foil out of the tin and peel away. Cut the biscuit into 24 pieces and arrange on a plate.

# Chocolate Dominoes

**Makes 16**

oil, for greasing

175g/6oz/¾ cup soft margarine

175g/6oz/⅞ cup caster (superfine) sugar

150g/5oz/⅔ cup self-raising (self-rising) flour

25g/1oz cocoa powder (unsweetened)

3 eggs

*For the Topping*

175g/6oz/¾ cup butter, softened

25g/1oz cocoa powder (unsweetened)

300g/11oz/3 cups icing (confectioners') sugar

a few liquorice strips and 115g/4oz packet M & M's, for decoration

1 Preheat the oven to 180°C/350°F/ Gas 4. Brush an 18 × 28cm/7 × 11in baking tin (pan) with a little oil and line with baking parchment.

2 Put all the cake ingredients in a bowl and beat until smooth.

3 Spoon into the tin and level the surface with a palette knife.

4 Bake in the oven for 30 minutes, or until the cake springs back when pressed with the fingertips.

5 Cool in the tin for 5 minutes, then loosen the edges with a knife and turn out on to a wire rack. Peel off the paper and allow the cake to cool.

6 Turn the cake on to a chopping board and cut into 16 bars.

7 To make the topping, place the butter in a bowl, sift in the cocoa and icing sugar and beat until smooth. Spread the topping evenly over the cakes with a palette knife.

8 Add a strip of liquorice to each cake, decorate with M & M's for domino dots and arrange the cakes on a serving plate.

**VARIATION**
**Traffic Light Cakes**
**Makes 16**
To make Traffic Light Cakes omit the cocoa and add an extra 25g/1oz/3 tbsp flour. Omit the cocoa from the icing and add an extra 25g/1oz/3 tbsp icing (confectioners') sugar and flavour with 2.5ml/½ tsp vanilla essence (extract). Spread over the cakes and decorate with eight halved red, yellow and green glacé (candied) cherries to look like traffic lights.

# Marshmallow Krispie Cakes

**Makes 45**

oil, for greasing

250g/9oz bag toffees

50g/2oz/4 tbsp butter

45ml/3 tbsp milk

115g/4oz marshmallows

175g/6oz Rice Krispies

1 Lightly brush a 20 × 33cm/8 × 13in roasting pan with a little oil. Put the toffees, butter and milk in a pan and heat gently, stirring until the toffees have melted.

2 Add the marshmallows and Rice Krispies and stir until well mixed and the marshmallows have melted.

3 Spoon into the pan, level the surface and leave to set. Cut into squares, put into paper cases and serve.

# Mini-muffins

**Makes 24**

200g/7oz/1½ cups plain (all-purpose) flour

10ml/2 tsp baking powder

50g/2oz/¼ cup soft light brown sugar

150ml/¼ pint/⅔ cup milk

1 egg, beaten

50g/2oz/4 tbsp butter or margarine, melted

50g/2oz glacé (candied) cherries

50g/2oz ready-to-eat dried apricots

2.5ml/½ tsp vanilla essence (extract)

1 Preheat the oven to 220°C/ 425°F/Gas 7 and place 24 petits fours cases in two mini patty tins (muffin pans).

2 Place the flour, baking powder and sugar in a bowl and add the milk, egg and melted butter or margarine. Stir thoroughly until the mixture is smooth.

3 Chop the cherries and apricots and stir into the muffin mixture with the vanilla essence.

4 Spoon the muffin mixture into the paper cases so they are about three-quarters full.

5 Cook for 10–12 minutes, until well risen and browned. If you have just one tin cook in two batches.

**TIP**
For older children, spoon the mixture into 12 medium-size muffin cases. Muffins are best served warm from the oven. If they aren't eaten immediately, they can be frozen for up to three months.

**VARIATIONS**
**Chocolate Chip Muffins**
Substitute 25g/1oz unsweetened cocoa powder for 25g/1oz/2 tbsp flour. Omit the cherries, apricots and vanilla and substitute 50g/2oz white and 50g/2oz plain (semisweet) chocolate dots.

**Orange and Banana Muffins**
Substitute 2 small mashed bananas for 60ml/2fl oz/¼ cup milk. Omit the cherries, apricot and vanilla, and add 15ml/1 tbsp grated orange rind.

# Bread Animals

**Makes 15**

oil, for greasing

2 × 280g/10oz packets white bread mix

a few currants (raisins)

½ small red (bell) pepper

1 small carrot

1 egg

1 Brush two large baking sheets with a little oil. Put the bread mixes in a large bowl and make up as directed on the packet, with warm water.

2 Knead on a lightly floured surface for 5 minutes, until the dough is smooth and elastic. Return the dough to the bowl, cover with oiled clear film (plastic wrap) and leave in a warm place for ¾–1 hour, until it has doubled in size.

3 Preheat the oven to 220°C/ 425°F/Gas 7. Knead the dough again for 5 minutes and then divide into five pieces.

4 To make snakes, take one piece of dough, cut into three and shape each into a 15cm/6in snake, making a slit in one end for the mouth. Twist the snakes on the baking sheet. Insert two currants for eyes. Cut out a thin strip of pepper, cutting a triangle at one end for the forked tongue.

5 For hedgehogs, take another piece of dough and cut into three. Shape each into an oval about 6cm/2½in long. Place on the baking sheet and add currant eyes and a red pepper nose. Snip the dough with scissors to make the prickly spines.

6 For the mice, take a third piece of dough and cut into four pieces. Shape three pieces into ovals, each about 6cm/2½in long and place on the baking sheet. Shape tiny rounds of dough for ears and wiggly tails from the fourth piece of dough. Press on to the mice bodies and use the currants for eyes.

7 Cut small strips of carrot and use for whiskers.

**TIP**

Give a portion of the prepared dough to your children, with some chopped dried fruits, and allow them to create their very own bread animals.

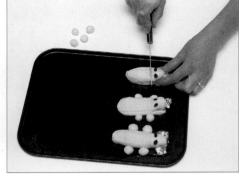

8 For the crocodiles, cut another piece of dough into three. Take a small piece off each and reserve. Shape the large pieces into 10cm/4in long sausages. Make slits for the mouths and wedge open with crumpled foil. Add currant eyes. Shape the spare dough into feet and press into position. Make criss-cross cuts on the backs.

9 For rabbits, take the final piece of dough and cut into three. Take a small piece off each for tails. Roll the remaining pieces of dough into thick sausages 18cm/7in long. Loop the dough and twist twice to form the body and head of rabbit. Use the rest for tails.

10 Cover the shapes with oiled clear film and leave in a warm place for 10–15 minutes. Brush with beaten egg and cook for 10–12 minutes, until golden.

11 Serve warm or cold, split and filled with ham or cheese.

# Cheese Shapes

**Makes 15**

oil, for greasing

350g/12oz/3 cups self-raising
  (self-rising) flour

pinch of salt

115g/4oz/½ cup margarine

115g/4oz Cheddar or mild cheese

2 eggs, beaten

60ml/4 tbsp milk

10ml/2 tsp sesame seeds

10ml/2 tsp poppy seeds

**1** Preheat the oven to 220°C/
425°F/Gas 7.

**2** Place the flour and salt in a
bowl, add the margarine and rub
in with your fingertips, or use an
electric mixer, until the mixture
resembles fine breadcrumbs.

**3** Grate the cheese, reserve 30ml/
2 tbsp and stir the rest into the
flour. Add three-quarters of the
beaten eggs and milk to the flour and
mix to a soft dough.

**4** Knead the dough lightly and roll
out thickly on a surface that has
been dusted with flour.

**5** Stamp out numbers with 7cm/3in
cutters and arrange well spaced
apart on two baking sheets. Re-roll
trimmings and stamp out more shapes
to use up the pastry.

**6** Brush the tops of the numbers
with the reserved egg. Sprinkle
five of the numbers with sesame
seeds, five with poppy seeds and the
remainder with grated cheese.

**7** Cook for 12–15 minutes, until
well risen and browned. Cool
slightly, then arrange the shapes on a
plate and serve warm.

# Marmite and Cheese Whirls

**Makes 16**

oil, for greasing

250g/9oz frozen puff pastry, defrosted

flour, for dusting

2.5ml/½ tsp Marmite

1 egg, beaten

50g/2oz Red Leicester, Cheddar or mild cheese, grated

carrot and cucumber sticks, to serve

1 Preheat the oven to 220°C/ 425°F/Gas 7 and brush a large baking sheet with a little oil.

2 Roll out the pastry on a floured surface to a large rectangle, about 35 × 25cm/14 × 10in.

3 Spread the pastry with Marmite, leaving a 1 cm/½in border. Brush the edges of the pastry with egg and sprinkle the cheese to cover the Marmite.

**TIP**
Omit the Marmite and use peanut butter if preferred. If the shapes become a little squashed when sliced, reform into rounds by opening out the layers with the end of a knife.

4 Roll the pastry up quite tightly like a Swiss roll (jelly roll), starting from a longer edge. Brush the outside of the pastry with beaten egg.

5 Cut the roll into thick slices and place on the baking sheet.

6 Cook for 12–15 minutes until the pastry is well risen and golden. Arrange on a serving plate and serve warm or cold with carrot and cucumber sticks.

# INDEX

# NUTRITIONAL INFORMATION

The nutritional analysis that follows is for the whole recipe.

**p14 Sticky Chicken** Energy 109Kcal/458kJ; Protein 14.7g; Carbohydrate 1.2g, of which sugars 1.1g; Fat 5.1g, of which saturates 1.4g; Cholesterol 77mg; Calcium 9mg; Fibre 0g; Sodium 222mg.

**p16 Coriander Chicken Casserole** Energy 157Kcal/658kJ; Protein 21.8g; Carbohydrate 7.6g, of which sugars 4.8g; Fat 4.6g, of which saturates 1g; Cholesterol 105mg; Calcium 38mg; Fibre 1.6g; Sodium 101mg.

**p16 Chicken and Cheese Parcels** Energy 252Kcal/1050kJ; Protein 27.6g; Carbohydrate 0.2g, of which sugars 0.2g; Fat 15.1g, of which saturates 6.5g; Cholesterol 87mg; Calcium 190mg; Fibre 0g; Sodium 436mg.

**p18 Peppered Beef Casserole** Energy 229Kcal/958kJ; Protein 18g; Carbohydrate 26.5g, of which sugars 8.2g; Fat 6.3g, of which saturates 2.3g; Cholesterol 33mg; Calcium 43mg; Fibre 3.3g; Sodium 251mg.

**p19 Lamb Stew** Energy 152Kcal/635kJ; Protein 12.3g; Carbohydrate 7.5g, of which sugars 5g; Fat 8.4g, of which saturates 3.3g; Cholesterol 44mg; Calcium 29mg; Fibre 2.2g; Sodium 59mg.

**p20 Mexican Beef** Energy 171Kcal/715kJ; Protein 9.5g; Carbohydrate 11.8g, of which sugars 2.9g; Fat 9.8g, of which saturates 3.9g; Cholesterol 23mg; Calcium 83mg; Fibre 1.7g; Sodium 275mg.

**p20 Lamb and Celery Casserole** Energy 142Kcal/596kJ; Protein 12.6g; Carbohydrate 8.4g, of which sugars 3.8g; Fat 6.8g, of which saturates 3.1g; Cholesterol 44mg; Calcium 33mg; Fibre 1.5g; Sodium 67mg.

**p22 Shepherd's Pie** Energy 388Kcal/1617kJ; Protein 21.7g; Carbohydrate 28.7g, of which sugars 11.9g; Fat 21.5g, of which saturates 10.3g; Cholesterol 69mg; Calcium 69mg; Fibre 4.5g; Sodium 382mg.

**p23 Tuna Fish Cakes** Energy 263Kcal/1104kJ; Protein 16.6g; Carbohydrate 19.4g, of which sugars 4.9g; Fat 13.9g, of which saturates 1.7g; Cholesterol 81mg; Calcium 80mg; Fibre 3.3g; Sodium 183mg.

**p24 Fish and Cheese Pies** Energy 300Kcal/1258kJ; Protein 19.3g; Carbohydrate 25.5g, of which sugars 6.5g; Fat 13.9g, of which saturates 7.8g; Cholesterol 59mg; Calcium 228mg; Fibre 1.6g; Sodium 246mg.

**p25 Surprise Fish Parcels** Energy 89Kcal/376kJ; Protein 17.9g; Carbohydrate 2.5g, of which sugars 2.4g; Fat 0.9g, of which saturates 0.2g; Cholesterol 32mg; Calcium 36mg; Fibre 1g; Sodium 670mg.

**p26 Cowboy Sausages and Beans** Energy 225Kcal/944kJ; Protein 9.8g; Carbohydrate 22.7g, of which sugars 8.4g; Fat 11.4g, of which saturates 4.1g; Cholesterol 15mg; Calcium 89mg; Fibre 5.4g; Sodium 702mg.

**p26 Mini Toad in the Hole** Energy 282Kcal/1183kJ; Protein 11.5g; Carbohydrate 28.3g, of which sugars 2.9g; Fat 14.6g, of which saturates 4.8g; Cholesterol 119mg; Calcium 131mg; Fibre 1.3g; Sodium 372mg.

**p28 Pork Hotpot** Energy 230Kcal/967kJ; Protein 21.4g; Carbohydrate 24.7g, of which sugars 7.4g; Fat 5.7g, of which saturates 1.6g; Cholesterol 55mg; Calcium 32mg; Fibre 2.5g; Sodium 134mg.

**p29 Pork and Lentil Casserole** Energy 369Kcal/1531kJ; Protein 17.7g; Carbohydrate 12.8g, of which sugars 5.2g; Fat 27.8g, of which saturates 9.9g; Cholesterol 63mg; Calcium 31mg; Fibre 2.1g; Sodium 65mg.

**p30 Sticky Ribs and Apple Slaw** Energy 454Kcal/1896kJ; Protein 23g; Carbohydrate 25.2g, of which sugars 16.4g; Fat 29.8g, of which saturates 8g; Cholesterol 86mg; Calcium 44mg; Fibre 2.1g; Sodium 357mg.

**p31 Mini Cheese and Ham Tarts** Energy 100Kcal/419kJ; Protein 3.2g; Carbohydrate 9.6g, of which sugars 1.3g; Fat 5.6g, of which saturates 1.2g; Cholesterol 21mg; Calcium 59mg; Fibre 0.4g; Sodium 101mg.

**p32 Pick-up Sticks** Energy 54Kcal/223kJ; Protein 1.7g; Carbohydrate 7.7g, of which sugars 6.9g; Fat 2g, of which saturates 0.3g; Cholesterol 0mg; Calcium 29mg; Fibre 2.3g; Sodium 318mg.

**p34 Spinach Pancakes with Ham and Cheese** Energy 265Kcal/1111kJ; Protein 11.7g; Carbohydrate 22g, of which sugars 5.5g; Fat 15g, of which saturates 5g; Cholesterol 89mg; Calcium 250mg; Fibre 1.2g; Sodium 325mg.

**p35 Cauliflower and Broccoli with Cheese** Energy 264Kcal/ 1101kJ; Protein 14.6g; Carbohydrate 11.9g, of which sugars 5.9g; Fat 17.6g, of which saturates 6.1g; Cholesterol 119mg; Calcium 293mg; Fibre 2.1g; Sodium 281mg.

**p36 Potato Boats** Energy 257Kcal/1073kJ; Protein 10.9g; Carbohydrate 24.7g, of which sugars 7.4g; Fat 13.4g, of which saturates 6.4g; Cholesterol 39mg; Calcium 165mg; Fibre 2.9g; Sodium 573mg.

**p37 Fat Cats** Energy 553Kcal/ 2308kJ; Protein 13.5g; Carbohydrate 46.6g, of which sugars 4.7g; Fat 36.8g, of which saturates 3.9g; Cholesterol 18mg; Calcium 258mg; Fibre 0.9g; Sodium 514mg.

**p38 Potato, Carrot and Courgette Rosti** Energy 37Kcal/ 155kJ; Protein 0.7g; Carbohydrate 5.2g, of which sugars 1g; Fat 1.6g, of which saturates 0.2g; Cholesterol 0mg; Calcium 5mg; Fibre 0.5g; Sodium 5mg.

**p38 Veggie Burgers** Energy 118Kcal/ 495kJ; Protein 4.1g; Carbohydrate 13.3g, of which sugars 2g; Fat 5.8g, of which saturates 1.7g; Cholesterol 54mg; Calcium 68mg; Fibre 1.4g; Sodium 54mg.

**p40 Vegetable Lasagne** Energy 296Kcal/1243kJ; Protein 11.7g; Carbohydrate 30.7g, of which sugars 8.6g; Fat 14.5g, of which saturates 8g; Cholesterol 33mg; Calcium 243mg; Fibre 2.9g; Sodium 210mg.

**p41 Aubergine Bolognaise** Energy 184Kcal/781kJ; Protein 8.2g; Carbohydrate 36.6g, of which sugars 9.6g; Fat 1.5g, of which saturates 0.4g; Cholesterol 0mg; Calcium 39mg; Fibre 4.9g; Sodium 58mg.

**p42 Speedy Chicken Pie** Energy 244Kcal/1015kJ; Protein 14.9g; Carbohydrate 7.5g, of which sugars 1.6g; Fat 17.2g, of which saturates 4.6g; Cholesterol 54mg; Calcium 68mg; Fibre 0.7g; Sodium 241mg.

**p44 Skinny Dippers** Energy 444Kcal/1870kJ; Protein 33.4g; Carbohydrate 45.9g, of which sugars 10g; Fat 15.1g, of which saturates 8.2g; Cholesterol 99mg; Calcium 160mg; Fibre 3g; Sodium 771mg.

**p45 Sweet and Sour Chicken** Energy 338Kcal/1409kJ; Protein 19.3g; Carbohydrate 29g, of which sugars 6.5g; Fat 16.3g, of which saturates 4.1g; Cholesterol 170mg; Calcium 53mg; Fibre 0.9g; Sodium 351mg.

**p46 Ham and Tomato Scramble** Energy 192Kcal/808kJ; Protein 15.7g; Carbohydrate 16.7g, of which sugars 4g; Fat 7.6g, of which saturates 2.1g; Cholesterol 211mg; Calcium 74mg; Fibre 1.2g; Sodium 638mg.

**p46 Ham Salad Clown** Energy 94Kcal/391kJ; Protein 8.5g; Carbohydrate 2.2g, of which sugars 2.2g; Fat 5.5g, of which saturates 3.2g; Cholesterol 46mg; Calcium 99mg; Fibre 0.2g; Sodium 398mg.

**p48 Spanish Omelette** Energy 130Kcal/546kJ; Protein 9.3g; Carbohydrate 9.9g, of which sugars 1.8g; Fat 6.4g, of which saturates 1.7g; Cholesterol 110mg; Calcium 22mg; Fibre 1.2g; Sodium 349mg.

**p49 Pasta with Ham Sauce** Energy 434Kcal/1814kJ; Protein 20g; Carbohydrate 37g, of which sugars 5.6g; Fat 23.6g, of which saturates 6.7g; Cholesterol 43mg; Calcium 310mg; Fibre 2.4g; Sodium 635mg.

**p50 Quickie Kebabs** Energy 59Kcal/248kJ; Protein 5.2g; Carbohydrate 3g, of which sugars 2.9g; Fat 3g, of which saturates 0.6g; Cholesterol 15mg; Calcium 6mg; Fibre 0.6g; Sodium 358mg.

**p50 Sausage Wrappers** Energy 272Kcal/1136kJ; Protein 20.4g; Carbohydrate 7.8g, of which sugars 2.8g; Fat 18g, of which saturates 5.7g; Cholesterol 137mg; Calcium 24mg; Fibre 0.8g; Sodium 1342mg.

**p52 Corned Beef Hash** Energy 222Kcal/931kJ; Protein 16.9g; Carbohydrate 18.1g, of which sugars 5g; Fat 9.6g, of which saturates 3.7g; Cholesterol 48mg; Calcium 34mg; Fibre 1.5g; Sodium 628mg.

**p53 Cannibal Necklaces** Energy 240Kcal/1003kJ; Protein 14.1g; Carbohydrate 19.5g, of which sugars 5.2g; Fat 12.2g, of which saturates 4.8g; Cholesterol 36mg; Calcium 231mg; Fibre 2.3g; Sodium 383mg.

**p54 Beef Burgers** Energy 305Kcal/1282kJ; Protein 16.3g; Carbohydrate 34.1g, of which sugars 4g; Fat 12.5g, of which saturates 5.1g; Cholesterol 35mg; Calcium 53mg; Fibre 2.5g; Sodium 222mg.

**p55 Four Fast Fishes** Energy 268Kcal/1124kJ; Protein 16.4g; Carbohydrate 27.1g, of which sugars 3.8g; Fat 11.2g, of which saturates 1.6g; Cholesterol 48mg; Calcium 99mg; Fibre 2.3g; Sodium 306mg.

**p56 Tuna Risotto** Energy 190Kcal/798kJ; Protein 15.8g; Carbohydrate 26.6g, of which sugars 3.7g; Fat 2.4g, of which saturates 0.4g; Cholesterol 26mg; Calcium 22mg; Fibre 1.7g; Sodium 243mg.

**p56 Fish Finger Log Cabins** Energy 99Kcal/414kJ; Protein 6.4g; Carbohydrate 9.3g, of which sugars 2.3g; Fat 4.3g, of which saturates 1.3g; Cholesterol 15mg; Calcium 81mg; Fibre 1.1g; Sodium 172mg.

**p58 Shape Sorters** Energy 300Kcal/1250kJ; Protein 12.2g; Carbohydrate 16.2g, of which sugars 2.6g; Fat 20.6g, of which saturates 7.4g; Cholesterol 24mg; Calcium 223mg; Fibre 1.5g; Sodium 416mg.

**p58 Happy Families** Energy 251Kcal/1051kJ; Protein 13.4g; Carbohydrate 22.2g, of which sugars 4.6g; Fat 12.7g, of which saturates 4.6g; Cholesterol 40mg; Calcium 229mg; Fibre 1.1g; Sodium 942mg.

**p60 French Toast Butterflies** Energy 243Kcal/1018kJ; Protein 17.2g; Carbohydrate 17g, of which sugars 3.9g; Fat 12g, of which saturates 5.2g; Cholesterol 127mg; Calcium 216mg; Fibre 2.4g; Sodium 615mg.

**p61 Tuna Flowers** Energy 384Kcal/1607kJ; Protein 17.4g; Carbohydrate 31.8g, of which sugars 4.3g; Fat 21.3g, of which saturates 11.6g; Cholesterol 63mg; Calcium 251mg; Fibre 2g; Sodium 600mg.

**p62 Noughts and Crosses** Energy 379Kcal/1578kJ; Protein 20.5g; Carbohydrate 15.4g, of which sugars 2.6g; Fat 25.4g, of which saturates 14.7g; Cholesterol 68mg; Calcium 462mg; Fibre 1.1g; Sodium 827mg.

**p62 Cheese Strips on Toast** Energy 273Kcal/1137kJ; Protein 15g; Carbohydrate 13.5g, of which sugars 0.9g; Fat 16.9g, of which saturates 10.9g; Cholesterol 49mg; Calcium 400mg; Fibre 0.5g; Sodium 503mg.

**p64 Speedy Sausage Rolls** Energy 91Kcal/378kJ; Protein 2.3g; Carbohydrate 7.1g, of which sugars 0.5g; Fat 6.1g, of which saturates 2.7g; Cholesterol 11mg; Calcium 19mg; Fibre 0.2g; Sodium 171mg.

**p65 Pizza Clock** Energy 204Kcal/856kJ; Protein 10g; Carbohydrate 23.2g, of which sugars 9.3g; Fat 8.1g, of which saturates 4.3g; Cholesterol 25mg; Calcium 173mg; Fibre 2.2g; Sodium 547mg.

**p66 Spotted Sandwiches** Energy 275Kcal/1151kJ; Protein 8.1g; Carbohydrate 28.2g, of which sugars 3.8g; Fat 15.3g, of which saturates 2.7g; Cholesterol 106mg; Calcium 107mg; Fibre 2.1g; Sodium 382mg.

**p66 Sandwich Snails** Energy 188Kcal/783kJ; Protein 6.6g; Carbohydrate 11.6g, of which sugars 2.9g; Fat 12.9g, of which saturates 4.6g; Cholesterol 24mg; Calcium 124mg; Fibre 0.8g; Sodium 345mg.

**p68 Fruit Fondue** Energy 197Kcal/833kJ; Protein 3.8g; Carbohydrate 33.7g, of which sugars 30.2g; Fat 5.4g, of which saturates 2.4g; Cholesterol 4mg; Calcium 107mg; Fibre 1.5g; Sodium 44mg.

**p70 Apple and Orange Fool** Energy 219Kcal/924kJ; Protein 5.5g; Carbohydrate 37.6g, of which sugars 23.8g; Fat 6.1g, of which saturates 3.8g; Cholesterol 21mg; Calcium 188mg; Fibre 2.1g; Sodium 117mg.

**p71 Peach Melba Dessert** Energy 153Kcal/650kJ; Protein 7g; Carbohydrate 30.8g, of which sugars 30.8g; Fat 1.3g, of which saturates 0.6g; Cholesterol 2mg; Calcium 238mg; Fibre 1.7g; Sodium 98mg.

**p72 Strawberry Ice Cream** Energy 2026Kcal/8391kJ; Protein 19.9g; Carbohydrate 101.4g, of which sugars 86.5g; Fat 169.2g, of which saturates 100.2g; Cholesterol 420mg; Calcium 606mg; Fibre 5.4g; Sodium 267mg.

**p73 Raspberry Sorbet** Energy 1055Kcal/4518kJ; Protein 10.6g; Carbohydrate 266.2g, of which sugars 266.2g; Fat 2g, of which saturates 0.7g; Cholesterol 0mg; Calcium 288mg; Fibre 16.9g; Sodium 34mg.

**p74 Yogurt Lollies** Energy 41Kcal/172kJ; Protein 1.9g; Carbohydrate 7.3g, of which sugars 7.3g; Fat 0.6g, of which saturates 0.4g; Cholesterol 2mg; Calcium 68mg; Fibre 0g; Sodium 27mg.

**p74 Jolly Jellies** Energy 195Kcal/824kJ; Protein 4.9g; Carbohydrate 39.2g, of which sugars 38.9g; Fat 3.2g, of which saturates 2g; Cholesterol 9mg; Calcium 55mg; Fibre 0.3g; Sodium 26mg.

**p76 Pancakes** Energy 285Kcal/1194kJ; Protein 8.1g; Carbohydrate 33.3g, of which sugars 19.9g; Fat 14.2g, of which saturates 6.1g; Cholesterol 66mg; Calcium 163mg; Fibre 1.5g; Sodium 78mg.

**p77 Traffic Light Sundaes** Energy 224Kcal/940kJ; Protein 4.3g; Carbohydrate 36.7g, of which sugars 36.6g; Fat 7.7g, of which saturates 4.5g; Cholesterol 0mg; Calcium 73mg; Fibre 0.5g; Sodium 41mg.

**p78 Cheat's Trifle** Energy 175Kcal/741kJ; Protein 4.7g; Carbohydrate 32.5g, of which sugars 26.2g; Fat 3.1g, of which saturates 0.3g; Cholesterol 2mg; Calcium 115mg; Fibre 0.9g; Sodium 73mg.

**p78 Baked Bananas** Energy 184Kcal/770kJ; Protein 2.9g; Carbohydrate 27g, of which sugars 25.1g; Fat 7.8g, of which saturates 4.6g; Cholesterol 0mg; Calcium 55mg; Fibre 0.9g; Sodium 31mg.

**p80 Orange and Apple Rockies** Energy 87Kcal/366kJ; Protein 1.3g; Carbohydrate 11.6g, of which sugars 4.5g; Fat 4.3g, of which saturates 0.9g; Cholesterol 8mg; Calcium 19mg; Fibre 0.5g; Sodium 42mg.

**p82 Mini Cup Cakes** Energy 31Kcal/130kJ; Protein 0.4g; Carbohydrate 3.5g, of which sugars 2.1g; Fat 1.8g, of which saturates 0.1g; Cholesterol 7mg; Calcium 9mg; Fibre 0.1g; Sodium 25mg.

**p83 Shortbread Shapes** Energy 28Kcal/117kJ; Protein 0.3g; Carbohydrate 3.2g, of which sugars 0.9g; Fat 1.7g, of which saturates 1g; Cholesterol 4mg; Calcium 4mg; Fibre 0.1g; Sodium 12mg.

**p84 Date Crunch** Energy 120Kcal/503kJ; Protein 1.3g; Carbohydrate 15.3g, of which sugars 10.1g; Fat 6.4g, of which saturates 3.6g; Cholesterol 12mg; Calcium 27mg; Fibre 0.4g; Sodium 85mg.

**p85 Chocolate Dominoes** Energy 335Kcal/1400kJ; Protein 2.9g; Carbohydrate 38.8g, of which sugars 31.3g; Fat 19.8g, of which saturates 6.4g; Cholesterol 59mg; Calcium 41mg; Fibre 0.7g; Sodium 199mg.

**p86 Marshmallow Krispie Cakes** Energy 56Kcal/235kJ; Protein 0.7g; Carbohydrate 9g, of which sugars 4.4g; Fat 2.2g, of which saturates 1.1g; Cholesterol 3mg; Calcium 39mg; Fibre 0g; Sodium 28mg.

**p86 Mini-muffins** Energy 67Kcal/281kJ; Protein 1.4g; Carbohydrate 11.1g, of which sugars 4.8g; Fat 2.2g, of which saturates 1.2g; Cholesterol 13mg; Calcium 25mg; Fibre 0.4g; Sodium 19mg.

**p88 Cup Cake Faces** Energy 328Kcal/1374kJ; Protein 3.2g; Carbohydrate 42.5g, of which sugars 33.1g; Fat 17.3g, of which saturates 5.4g; Cholesterol 43mg; Calcium 53mg; Fibre 0.6g; Sodium 127mg.

**p89 Gingerbread People** Energy 94Kcal/395kJ; Protein 1.2g; Carbohydrate 16.5g, of which sugars 9.3g; Fat 3g, of which saturates 0.7g; Cholesterol 0mg; Calcium 19mg; Fibre 0.4g; Sodium 23mg.

**p90 Bread Animals** Energy 147Kcal/624kJ; Protein 4.7g; Carbohydrate 28.5g, of which sugars 1.8g; Fat 2.4g, of which saturates 0.4g; Cholesterol 13mg; Calcium 55mg; Fibre 1.4g; Sodium 139mg.

**p92 Cheese Shapes** Energy 184Kcal/769kJ; Protein 5.2g; Carbohydrate 18.2g, of which sugars 0.4g; Fat 10.4g, of which saturates 2g; Cholesterol 33mg; Calcium 100mg; Fibre 0.8g; Sodium 127mg.

**p93 Marmite and Cheese Whirls** Energy 76Kcal/318kJ; Protein 2.1g; Carbohydrate 5.8g, of which sugars 0.2g; Fat 5.2g, of which saturates 0.8g; Cholesterol 15mg; Calcium 34mg; Fibre 0g; Sodium 82mg.